THE LITTLE BOOK OF

Cigars

Éric Deschodt

Flammarion

QUESTIONS

For nearly two centuries the Havana cigar has been considered the king of cigars, and Cuba has basked in the light of its renown.
What makes Cuban cigars so special? What are the other noteworthy cigar-producing countries?

Every cigar provides a unique pleasure, and there is a great variety of shapes, sizes, aromas, colors, and tastes. So how does one choose a cigar?
What are the rules of cigar etiquette?

Whether they love them or loathe them, enjoy them, or avoid them, people have always felt strongly about cigars.
Which celebrities have been instrumental in shaping the cigar's image?

A N S W E R S

Orientation p. 6

The alphabetical entries have been classified according to the following categories. Each category is indicated with a small colored square.

■ Types of Cigars:
Origins
Characteristics

■ Cigars and Life:
Fabrication
Enjoyment

■ History:
Historical facts
Economic contexts
Aficionados

The information given in each entry, together with cross-references indicated by asterisks, enables the reader to explore the world of cigars.

The Story of Cigars p. 10

The Story of Cigars provides a detailed overview of the themes and information provided in the alphabetical entries.

Alphabetical Guide p. 28

The entries, arranged in alphabetical order, tell you all you need to know to find your way around this fascinating world. The information is enriched with detailed discussion of the main cigar-producing countries, historical information, and essential savoir-faire for connoisseurs.

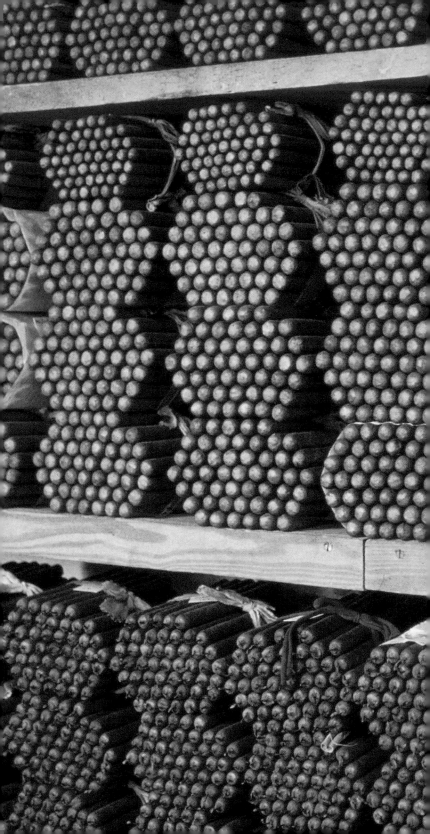

ORIENTATION

I. THE STORY OF CIGARS

A. Cigar Countries

Cuba is cigar country. The climate and soil are ideal for growing the best tobacco. Yet a century after they first discovered the island, Europeans were growing tobacco throughout the world and Cuba lost its exclusivity. Other countries brought out new blends and brands and the universe of cigars became all the richer.

■ *Altadis*	■ *Havana Tobacco*	■ *Southeast Asia*
■ *Brazil*	■ *Honduras*	■ *Transplantation History*
■ *Cuba*	■ *Italy*	■ *United States*
■ *Cuban Brands*	■ *Manila*	■ *Vintage*
■ *Dominican Republic*	■ *Revolution and Production*	■ *Vuelta Abajo*
■ *Dutch Cigars*	■ *Seville*	

B. The Art of Rolling

Cuban cigar manufacture is universally praised. *Tabaqueros* from the Dominican Republic are also known to be excellent. From seed to box, cigar production requires a number of skills. Cuba's *Escogida* festival celebrates the moment when cultivated tobacco leaves are passed from the planters into the expert hands of strippers and rollers.

■ *Blending*	■ Escogida	■ *Secret*
■ *Box*	■ *Fermentation*	■ *Stripping and Strippers*
■ *Bundling*	■ *Finca*	■ Tabaquero *or* Tabaquera
■ *Composition*	■ *Humidity*	■ *Tools*
■ *Cultivation*	■ *Plant*	■ *Warehouse Storage*
■ *Dominican Republic*	■ *Production Overview*	
■ *Drying*	■ *Rolling and Rollers*	

II. CIGAR MYSTIQUE

A. Smoking

How can you be sure to get maximum pleasure from your cigar? These entries provide valuable information on choosing and storing, as well as practical tips and pointers on how to experience nuances of aroma and taste.

B. The Cigar's Image

From the distribution of cigars upon the birth of a child to the condemned man's request for a last smoke, cigar smoking is viewed in vastly different ways. While the stereotypes of cigar-smoking capitalists and backroom politicians remain, the true cigar aficionado is not such a caricature but is more likely to be an epicure or even an aesthete.

III. DISCOVERING THE CIGAR

A. From Columbus to Castro

When Columbus first came upon the Arawak Indians, they were carrying "smoking cones" of tobacco, the distinguished ancestors of the contemporary cigar. Cigars acquired their contemporary form some three hundred years later, in Spain. Havana cigars took on their internationally recognized cachet in the nineteenth century.

- Discovery
- **Dutch Cigars**
- Etymology
- First Reported Smokers

- **Havana History**
- **Manufacture Begins Internationally**
- Revolution and Production

- Sailors
- **Seville**
- Smoking Room

B. King Havana

The Cuban Revolution shook up the cigar world, causing the end of some brands and the expansion of finer cigar tobacco cultivation into other countries. But the Cuban cigar industry is still going strong, as are brands from other lands.

- Altadis
- **Cigarillo**
- Cuban Brands
- Davidoff, Zino
- Dunhill, Alfred

- Gérard Père & Fils
- **La Escepion**
- **Montecristo**
- **Number**
- Revolution and Production

- **Romeo y Julieta**
- **Ring**
- **Seal**

THE STORY OF CIGARS

Today's cigar is a long-standing luxury. It started out in Seville,* Spain, in 1731: one hundred years later, almost all the top Havana brands were already in existence in Cuba,* home to the world's finest cigars. Cigars enjoyed great popularity in Europe in the nineteenth century, but were supplanted by cigarettes in the period between the two World Wars. Cigars are associated with luxury, but have, in fact, always been smoked by people from all walks of life, regardless of their bank accounts. From the lofty, pricey *puro,* made of only choice tobacco leaves from a single growing area, to the ever-popular, inexpensive cigarillo, which is made from tobacco scraps and is thus technically not a cigar, there is a type to fit virtually every taste and budget.

I. The Making of a Cigar
A. Cigar Countries

Tobacco is indigenous to the Americas. It was brought back to Europe by the first explorers in the fifteenth century, and transplanted over the five continents, wherever colonialism ventured. Although tobacco requires both high levels of humidity* and low rainfall to flourish, it took root throughout the Americas, Asia,* and parts of Europe. Cuba is a tobacco-grower's dream. This country has consistently produced the world's finest cigar tobacco. The greatest of the great Cuban tobacco comes from the outlying areas of the town of Pinar del Rio, far on the west of the island. Vuelta Abajo,* a stretch of under a hundred thousand acres (4,000 hectares), has a soil and climate perfect for producing superior tobacco leaves. Their quality has never been equaled elsewhere, despite centuries of concerted and ingenious attempts. The Spanish and Portuguese invaders of the sixteenth century got an early start, and spread tobacco growing throughout the region. Today, tobacco is also a thriving and highly lucrative crop in the Dominican Republic,* with a high-quality, high-volume yield. In Brazil,* the state of Bahia is the number one tobacco-producing area. Brazilian tobacco is black and potent. Tobacco is grown in every country throughout Central America, with Honduran* tobacco being the finest. Mexico's tobacco plantations are located primarily in the Yucatan. Further north, the United States* is the number one cigar-producing country in terms of volume. The main tobacco-producing states are North and South Carolina and Virginia. American tobacco is mild, and American cigars usually have flavor added.

In Asia, tobacco is cultivated in Burma, the Philippines, and Indonesia, where it was introduced by the Spanish, Dutch, and Portuguese invaders. Tobacco is also grown in a few southern European countries. They include Spain, the Bergerac region of south-west France, Tuscany in Italy, and the Balkans. These countries produce their own cigars as well.

B. The Art of Rolling

Tobacco needs heat and humidity* to grow. Its worst enemy is rain, but it requires a constant humidity level of about eighty percent. On the Cuban *fincas,** or farms and plantations where tobacco is raised, the seeds are sown in nurseries in September. Usually about

Tobacco field in Cuba.

a month later they are transplanted to fields. Harvest extends from January to March. The leaves are picked by hand, one by one, each when it is perfectly mature.

Making a fine cigar is a great art. The cigar is made up of three parts: wrapper, binder, and filler (see Composition). Each of the parts uses different leaves. Some plantations specialize in wrapper leaves, while others are devoted to filler leaves. Even on a single plant, what tobacco leaves will be used for differs according to their position on the plant, their level of exposure to sunlight, and the time they are picked. Before selling leaves to cigar factories, planters sort, dry,* and ferment* them. The leaves are then shown to the factory buyers during the *Escogida** festival.

Cigar Factory
in Cuba.
Photograph by
Henri Cartier-
Bresson. 1982.

After being selected by the buyers, tobacco leaves undergo a second and often a third fermentation. Cigar-making itself then begins, with stripping,* which is the removal of the tough central vein. The next step is blending,* where different leaves are mixed to give a cigar its individual character. This important step is followed by the actual cigar making. Stripped and blended leaves are given to the rollers,* who work with a special miniature machete-like knife called the *chaveta* (see Tools). Once they are rolled, the cigars are tied in bundles* and stored* in cedar cabinets for additional maturation before they are boxed.* Well-documented though it may be, there is always a secret* something involved in cigar making which remains a mystery, and is never divulged to outsiders.

II. CIGAR MYSTIQUE
A. Smoking

Although the choice of a cigar is a matter of taste and depends first and foremost on the individual smoker, certain cigars are right for different times of day and occasions. There are morning, afternoon, and evening cigars. Some are light and others heavy. Some take longer to smoke than others. It takes at least an hour to smoke a real cigar, and the larger models may take two hours to finish.

Cigar smoking begins with choosing* a cigar, which is not always a simple matter. There is a wide range of great cigars to choose from, and once a cigar is decided upon, there is still the question of which size,* model,* shape, and weight to select. Cigars are categorized by their place of origin, color* (which is largely a matter of aesthetics; not related to the cigar's flavor in general), taste,* which depends on the tobacco blends used, and price.* A *puro's* cost is relative to its origin. The world's greatest tobacco comes from a geographically small area, and there is only a finite amount of it to be had. In addition, certain excep-tional harvests make a particular year's vintage* more valuable. The world's finest cigars are all entirely hand-crafted; the richest, smoothest, and most aromatic cigars are Cuban Havanas. Next to Havanas, other

Following pages:
Winston
Churchill in his
office.
Photograph by
Cecil Beaton.
1940.

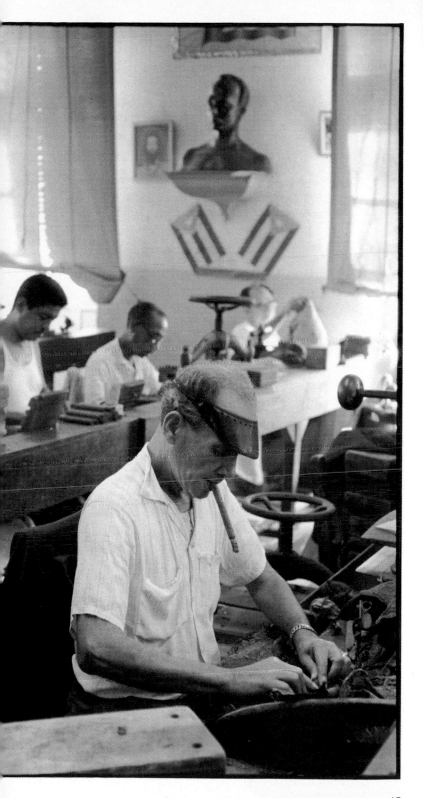

cigars are either harsher, more pungent, or just plain tasteless. They are also less expensive, and in fact preferable to some palates that prefer a milder or stronger taste. For Americans, the allure of Havanas is added to by the fact that, as a result of the trade embargo in effect since the 1959 Cuban Revolution,* Cuban cigars are not legally available in the United States.

The selected cigar must be cut to create an opening in the top for smoke to pass through. A whole range of accessories* has been invented over the years to do the job. After cutting comes lighting,* a delicate operation to be undertaken with precision and an odor-free match or lighter. Good burning* depends on proper lighting. The long blue-gray cigar ash* is an object of fascination for some aficionados,* and of debate for others. Should the ash be tipped, or left to fall into the ashtray on its own? The heady, thick cigar smoke* is of course another major by-product.

For many, the perfect time to enjoy a fine cigar is after a delicious meal. Like fine after-dinner liqueurs (see Alcohol) cigars can go hand in hand with fine food.* Also like outstanding wines and spirits, the best cigars mature over the years, and sometimes reach their point of perfection only after several years in storage.*

All smoking is a health hazard, but cigar smoking seems to be the least unhealthy form of smoking, since the smoke is not inhaled, and the nicotine level of the best cigar tobacco is especially low.

B. The Cigar's Image

The cigar has been associated with the image* of the ugly, arrogant capitalist, blinded by smoke rings of voracious greed, and ruthlessly blowing fumes into the faces of anyone who disagrees with him. To set the record straight, it should be pointed out that other objects, truly inaccessible to all but the wealthy few, make better symbols of conspicuous consumption. It has already been mentioned that cigars come in every price range. A fine cigar can cost about the same as a movie ticket, and provide an aficionado with the same amount of lasting enjoyment.

III. DISCOVERING THE CIGAR
A. From Columbus to Castro

The cigar has more than five hundred years of history behind it. The first Europeans to see a cigar were members of Christopher Columbus's expedition in 1492. When they set foot in what is now Cuba, they noticed that the natives were holding "half burning sticks." The original inhabitants of today's West Indies, as well as all of Central America, Mexico, and Brazil,* smoked cigars. The first reported smokers* of European origin were among the early explorers of the New World. Sailors* from the crews of these and subsequent expeditions helped spread tobacco use in their home countries. Spain was the first among them, followed by Portugal. André Thevet was one of the first to introduce tobacco plants to European soil; a Franciscan monk, he brought tobacco seeds back from a voyage to Brazil in 1556. Before the cigar caught on, Europeans initially smoked their tobacco in pipes. With its colonial control of Cuba, Spain set up a monopoly on tobacco and tobacco products. The Spanish authorities chose the southern city of Seville,* a port for trade with the West Indies, for the handling and processing of all tobacco. It was in Seville that first snuff, and, by the end of the seventeenth century, cigars, were manufactured. Cigar-smoking became popular in Spain, and the plantations back in Cuba expanded. In the eighteenth century, Cuba was granted permission by Spain to process a portion of the tobacco grown

Fidel Castro in Cuba. Photograph by Elliot Erwitt, 1964.

Following pages: Christen Schjellerup Købke (1810–1848), *The Cigar Seller.* Musée du Louvre, Paris.

21

Label from a
Havana
cigar box.

locally. The first factories opened. At the end of the century, the cigar as it is known today was invented in Seville and called the *puro* (pure). A *puro* is made only of tobacco leaves. Previously, the wrapper layers for cigars were made with non-tobacco leaves. The international popularity of the cigar was a result of the Spanish War of Independence (1808–1814). Cigars instantly caught on with British and French armies fighting on Spanish territory, and soldiers spread their newfound smoking habits throughout Europe. In London society circles, cigars were popular among the elegant dandies,* and luxuriously appointed smoking rooms* appeared in every fashionable place in London. Just as "stogie" came to be a generic name for all cigars in the United States,* the name deriving from the cigar plant in Conestoga, Pennsylvania, Cuban cigars came to be called Havanas, as their superior quality became universally recognized. Havanas won all the medals at the International and World Expositions that were so important for commerce up through the First World War. In these competitions, Havanas far outstripped contenders from the Caribbean, Brazil, and the Philippines, and left their machine-made poor relations from the Netherlands,* Germany, Belgium, and the United States in the dust. Today, industrial cigar making has diminished, but the market for hand-crafted cigars from Cuba and the Dominican Republic* is limited only by the land's finite ability to yield tobacco crops.

Tobacco being
dried in Java.

24

B. King Havana

Cigars are sold according to their brand.* The brand is a reflection on each cigar's quality. Shortly after taking control of Cuba, Fidel Castro set this time-honored tradition on its head when he decided to discontinue all the individual Havana brands and form one State cigar brand. Castro saw the brands as the trappings of a capitalism that had to be abolished. This move immediately devastated cigar exports, and Castro quickly reestablished the individual brands in order to save his country's economy. It took several years of reorganization after the 1959 Revolution for cigar quality to regain its superior level, and some of the greatest pre-Revolutionary brands, such as Henry Clay, never made it into the new era. But today the top brands distributed by the State tobacco company, Habanos S. A., stand up in quality to their former glory. These great brands include Bolivar, Montecristo,* Partagas, Punch, Romeo y Julieta,* and Sancho Panza. Castro founded Cohiba, a state brand, with the intention of making it the world's finest. Whether it is the absolute best is a question of taste, but no one would deny that it is an excellent cigar.

Cigar merchants play an important role in cigar distribution. The great cigar purveyors don't necessarily make cigars, but they store and sell them with genuine devotion. Dunhill* in London, Davidoff* and, more recently, Gérard & Fils in Geneva have founded, upheld, and perpetuated a tradition of the aficionado cigar merchant. Their staff is made up of connoisseurs dedicated to sharing their expertise with customers.

In 1998, American Consolidated Cigar Holdings as well as Hav-A-Tampa were acquired by the French company Seita, which subsequently completed a merger with Tabacalera of Spain in 2001. The resulting concern, known as Altadis,* is currently the world's largest cigar producer. While the majority of their cigars and cigar products cater to everyday standard tastes and market demand, Altadis also produces premium cigars and, along with the Cuban government, co-owns the Cuban cigar distribution company Habanos S.A.

Louis Armstrong, Billy Kyle, and Gerry Mulligan in New York.
Photograph by Dennis Stock, 1958.

■ ACCESSORIES
CUTTER AND CASE

In theory, all you need to smoke a cigar is a match. The head, or sealed rounded end, can be easily opened with a fingernail or teeth. This is the preferred method in Cuba, and is used by many a cigar-lover throughout the world. But biting is practical only in

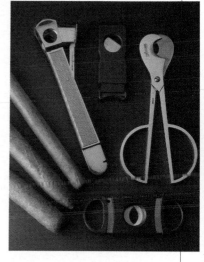

the tropics, where humidity preserves the natural elasticity of the tobacco leaves. In drier climates a special tool is often used to avoid damaging the cigar. The cigar cutter comes in a variety of forms. A sharp little pocket-knife version lets the smoker choose the opening size, tailoring its dimensions for an easy or tight draw.* Cigar scissors, with their incurving, slightly beveled blades, guard against ruining the wrapper* by cutting through the entire surface at once. There are also various guillotine or chopper models. Dihedral-blade "cat eye" cutters which make wedge cut V-shaped edges are to be avoided, because they damage the cigar head unless sharpened to perfection. Little cigar drills, which once did a fine job, have dropped out of favor. Lances, designed to improve the draw by penetrating into the cigar, can dig several inches into the filler,* but prove ineffectual because

the whole length of the cigar would need to be pierced to do the trick.
The most useful of all cigar accessories is actually the cigar case, which makes for good conservation. The humidity* in Cuba† makes it possible to carry *puros* (see Havana) loose in your pocket, but this is not generally the case elsewhere. In Europe and much of the United States, humidors,* or cigar humidifiers, are needed. Even with a quality humidor, cigars can dry out with time, causing the wrapper to open up, crumble, or crack.

■ Aficionado

The image of the cigar-smoking capitalist, which emerged during the Industrial Revolution of the nineteenth century, may never be lived down, despite the well-known cigar-loving habits of such leftist heroes as Che Guevera and Fidel Castro (see Revolution).

While Thomas Marshall, vice president under Woodrow Wilson, is remembered for having proclaimed to the United States Senate: "What this country really needs is a good five-cent cigar," and Winston Churchill relishes a cigar in some of the best-known photographs of this great English statesman, many politicians over the years have scrupulously avoided puffing in public. Presidents Bill Clinton and John F. Kennedy are among this number.

Cultural figures, from Mark Twain to Luciano Pavarotti, sports stars such as Babe Ruth, Lou Gehrig, and Michael Jordan, and film celebrities from Groucho Marx, Orson Welles, and Marlene Dietrich to Robert De Niro, Stanley Kubrick, and Demi Moore have, unlike politicians, tended to flaunt their cigar smoking.

Following pages:
Philippe-Jacques
Linder,
*The Train of
Pleasure.*
Late nineteenth
century.
Engraving. Musée
Carnavalet, Paris.

■ Alcohol

Drinking and cigar smoking make a perfect pair. For Cubans and sailors,* cigars go hand in hand with rum. In the United States and Europe, cigars and alcohol are seen as perfectly complementary. An after-dinner drink, such as cognac, is a wonderful example; other fine choices include port, brandy, scotch, bourbon, or strong ale. Havana cigars are so well-suited to wine that Davidoff* has named cigars after classic Bordeaux vintages and champagnes. But, beware, a the richness of a fine cigar will accentuate the flaws of a mediocre drink. There is much enjoyment to be had from experimenting with different cigar and alcohol combinations, and connoisseurs' published findings lend a scientific edge to the experiment. But when it comes down it, mixing a fine alcoholic beverage with a superb cigar is always a sure bet.

■ Altadis

On October 6, 1999, two tobacco giants—the French company Seita and the Spanish Tabacalera—announced their plans to merge, creating the biggest cigar company in the world, baptized Altadis.

Seita, the formerly state-owned French tobacco company, was established in 1926 as an organization to reimburse public debt. It was based on a royal monopoly reinstituted by Napoleon after the French Revolution. Indeed, the company's plant in Morlaix, Brittany, is still located in the original building constructed before the French Revolution, during the reign of Louis XV.

There had been a similar tobacco monopoly operating in the kingdoms of Castilla and Leon from 1636. Tabacalera S.A., the Spanish government monopoly, was established in 1945. The two companies, Tabacalera and Seita, expanded in parallel, developing new products such as the Voltigeur, a long and distinctive model made with a coarse Brazilian filler blend,* and the Picaduro (the only cigar made from exclusively French tobacco). In 1997, the Tabacalera Cigars International (TCI) subsidiary was created as a means of expanding in the United States,* Central America, and the Caribbean. TCI purchased Havatampa, Max Rohr, Tabacalera San Cristobal de Honduras and Tabacalera San Cristobal de Nicaragua, and thus became the world leader in the cigar market.

The merger between the two companies was prompted by a legal dispute over ownership of the exclusive Montecristo

An American cigar smoker, 1938.

FUMEURS

E. MESPLÈS
1163

See what a pestiferous and wicked poison from the devil it is.
It has happened several times to me only to smell it while going along
the road, in the provinces of Guatemala and Nicaragua, or entering
into the house of some Indian who had taken the smoke,
which in the Mexican language is called tobacco,
and suddenly smelling the violent stench, I was forced to leave with speed.

Girolamo Benzoni, 1541

label. Seita had come to an agreement with Cuba whereby it manufactured cigarillos made with Cuban tobacco, using the famous trademark, but Tabacalera claimed the brand name was its property. The result of the merger to resolve the long-drawn-out court case has been the creation of a group with twenty thousand employees present in some thirty-five countries, the world leader in cigars.

▣ Anti-Smoking

One of the best known and earliest anti-smoking tracts is the *Counterblast to Tobacco*, written in 1605 by James I of England himself. He was raised in the court of Queen Elizabeth I, where even the ladies in waiting took to smoking pipes in honor of Sir Walter Raleigh, who had popularized tobacco. Contrary to the medical opinion of his contemporaries, which attributed curative properties to tobacco, King James considered it a poison. "Smoking is a custom loathsome to the eye, hateful to the nose, harmful to the brain, dangerous to the lungs, and in the black, stinking fume thereof nearest resembling the horrible Stygian smoke of the pit that is bottomless." King James cited evidence that autopsies found smokers' "inward parts . . . infected with an oily kind of soot." James also said if he ever had the Devil to dinner, he would offer him a pipe. With regard to second-hand smoke, James asserted, "The wife must either take up smoking or resolve to live in a perpetual stinking torment." King James's was the first government to tax tobacco, which proved highly profitable.

The seventeenth century saw a gradual prohibition of tobacco throughout the world, when only a few countries, including France and Spain, saw fit to tax rather than ban it. In the nineteenth century another English monarch and guardian of morality, Queen Victoria, championed the anti-cigar lobby. Smoking in her presence or even anywhere where she might conceivably go was strictly forbidden. Over the course of the twentieth century, particularly in its final decades, tobacco's reputation went from bad to worse.

▣ Ash

For many smokers, cigar ash is a subject of fascination and philosophizing. Blue in color and relatively dense in texture, the solid nature of cigar ash allows it to accumulate on the end for over an inch before having to be tipped. In fact, there is no need to shake a cigar to make the ash fall prematurely, nor is there any point in trying to keep it as long as possible. Leaving the ash on too long obstructs air flow and can cause irregular burning. As a general rule, the better a cigar has been made the longer it can practically sustain its ash.

Once it begins to give off too much heat and leaves an aftertaste in the mouth, it is time to put the cigar down. Cigars don't have to be put out like cigarettes. A cigar stops burning by itself in the ashtray.

Cuban cigar workshop, 1990.

Nostalgia-prone aficionados may be tempted to leave the ash in the ashtray as a loving reminder of their last smoke. But harsh reality dictates that it be thrown away promptly, to avoid impregnating the room with the stench of cold tobacco, which eventually proves unappealing to even the most ardent cigar lovers.

■ Blending

Blending tobaccos is the main way that a cigar's personality is created. A brand's* success depends upon the consistency of its blends. It takes a savvy combining of leaves to ensure consistent taste* year after year. The reliability of any given vitola* resides with a master blender's ability to perpetuate consistent cigar strength, richness, aroma, and taste, year after year. Cuban and Dominican* tobaccos can be extremely rich. To experience their harmonious combinations is a delectable wonder every time. A master blender trains for years before taking on this responsibility, but it requires a natural gift as well.

A premium cigar requires the marrying of one excellent tobacco plant's* lower leaves with another's higher leaves. Lower leaves receive less sun, while the sun-drenched upper leaves are the richest and most flavorful. Meanwhile the leaves from a plant that are not used for one cigar are available for use in different combinations for other cigars. The filler contributes most to a cigar's taste because it comprises the largest part. Rollers* are given a basic formula for the cigar they have to make, and their expert eyes and dexterous hands provide the final insurance of quality and consistency.

35

■ Box

Havana boxes are made of Cuban cedar, an odorless, porous wood that allows the contents to breathe. A traditional "flat top" box holds twenty-five cigars in two layers: thirteen on the bottom and twelve on the top. They are separated by a cedar leaf "spacer" and lined up to display the rings and hide the veins that can mar the wrapper's smooth appearance. There are also cube-shaped cedar "cabinet" selection boxes which hold twenty-five, fifty, or, occasionally, a hundred cigars in bundles usually fastened with yellow ribbon. Certain specially out-sized cigars, such as the José Gener Magnum are boxed and sold individually. Other large yet more modest models,* including Davidoff's* Dom Pérignon, come in boxes of ten. The boxes are often elaborately decorated, with the brand name proudly proclaimed on the inside in prominent letters.

Medals won in nineteenth-century competitions at the great international and universal exhibitions are reproduced in vivid detail on the sides. Within, the cigars are almost always covered with a sheet of printed paper depicting colorful mythological, or historical, or pastoral themes. These are called "vistas" (views) and are sought after by collectors. In Cuba, vistas and cigar rings are exclusively designed and distributed by the Government

Printing Office in Havana. On the bottom of the box, three inscriptions appear on separate lines: "Habanos S.A.," "Hecho in Cuba," (made in Cuba) and "Totalmente a mano" (entirely handmade). The inscriptions must be heat stamped or engraved. Inscriptions can be gray, black, or gold in color. If they are simply inked on, the cigars are counterfeit. Since, in the United States, the real thing is not allowed, fakes are rather common.

Antique cigar box. Private collection, United States.

■ BRAZIL

Tobacco was grown in Brazil by the Portugese for export to Lisbon beginning in 1548. Ever since, Brazil has been at the forefront of cigar and tobacco production.

One of the first Westerners to report on tobacco, smoked by the ingenious peoples of the New World, was the French Franciscan, Friar André Thevet. He claimed to be the first to transplant *Nicotiana tabacum* from Brazil; though many dispute this. In 1568, Thevet wrote a description of the people of Brazil who smoked to cleanse the "superfluous humours of the brain." The friar followed suit.

Certain experts and aficionados* over the centuries have not hesitated to declare black-colored Brazilian cigars the only ones comparable to their Cuban counterparts. Brazilian flavor strikes a winning balance between robust body and mildness.

The oldest and biggest tobacco plantations of Brazil are in the coastal state of Bahia. Leaves cultivated here are used for wrappers, binders, and filler (see Composition). They are smaller than Cuban leaves. Mata Fina, with its top-quality Cruz das Almas and Conceicao do Almeida leaves, is black-colored. The soil lacks certain nutrients for the leaves to develop completely, but this makes for especially rich aroma. The black tobacco of this area produces mild, well-balanced cigars. They are so highly regarded that other quality tobaccos are routinely transported into the two towns in order to claim their appellations—this has earned them the name "railroad leaves."

Danneman Espada cigars are exported in see-through plastic boxes of twenty-five, and Danneman Vera Cruz comes in boxes of ten. Davidoff's* Brazilian models* include the Zino Santos and the Por Favor. The German Suerdick brand is the favorite of former Chancellor Helmut Kohl.

Bahia tobacco is used in the majority of American and European cigars.

* BRASILLO *

Bundles of
Havanas in a
Cuban factory.

■ Bundling

Rolled cigars are bound in bundles of fifty and tied with a (usually yellow) silk ribbon. Each bundle is called a "half wheel," based on the Cuban saying that on his or her fiftieth birthday a person has run half the wheel of life. The bundles are stored in cabinets or huge drawers made of Cuban cedar, a wood ideally suited for cigar preservation. They "rest" there from four to eight weeks in order to cool down after their third fermentation* and dry out slightly from the increased humidity* necessary for the production process. After this storage period comes the final round of quality control inspections. Cigars are individually examined, and one random cigar from each bundle is removed to be cut open and checked from the inside out. Next comes the last sorting based on color,* the affixing of cigar rings,* and boxing.

Burning

Regular and consistent combustion is, along with strength, flavor, and aroma, one of the most important qualities in a cigar. A great cigar always draws well. With proper lighting,* it burns evenly through and through, making smoking an effortless pleasure. Combustion is mainly a function of the filler leaves' quality, as well their density and the skill with which they have been combined in rolling.* This in turn is partly dependent on the binder and the precision with which it has been made to encase the filler. The wrapper, aside from providing a cigar with its visual and tactile characteristics, is also of importance for good burning (see Composition). A poorly rolled cigar of uneven density draws* badly. Burning will be concentrated either in the middle, to one side, or along the edges. A well-made cigar's three main parts—wrapper, binders, and filler—burn simultaneously. This is achieved through the perfect blending of at least three types of tobacco leaves that burn at different rates. The various-sized leaves come from three separate parts of the plant:* *volado* near the bottom (mild), *seco* in the middle (medium and most abundant leaves) and *ligero* (small, thick, and strongest-flavored leaves) at the top.

A cigar's thickness influences the draw, with wider cigars burning more slowly than thin ones.

Choosing a Cigar

The choice of cigar depends on the personality of the smoker, his or her mood, and the moment. Most cigar aficionados* have a favorite cigar size.*

A Davidoff Corona burning.

The moment is of primary importance since cigars are made to be enjoyed in peace, and require at least an hour to be fully savored. First of all, a cigar requires careful inspection since its quality can be evaluated in terms of the wrapper's color* and texture. If you slide your finger along it lengthwise, or press it lightly at various points, there should be no rustling or crackling. A fine specimen should be firm and give slightly when squeezed. Savoring its qualities continues with meticulous cutting and lighting before smoking proper begins.

Fundamental questions of taste include cigar size: short or long, fat or thin. There is also color to consider, ranging from very light through reddish to darker browns, to almost black. A cigar's freshness should be verified by looking into a box* of the selected brand.* A quick once-over will eliminate cigars whose wrappers are marred by leaf veins or stains.

Whitish spots of surface mold are common in the tropics, where fine cigars are made, and should not scare away a prospective smoker. With exposure to proper humidity

smokers. Ironically, Churchill was a direct descendant of the Duke of Marlborough. John Churchill, Duke of Marlborough was an officer in the Spanish War of Independence (see Seville), and the cigarette brand is named after him. Winston Churchill fell in love with the *puro* at the age of twenty-six. He was stationed in Havana as a war correspondent for the *Daily Graphic* on a salary of twenty-five pounds per article. Cuba was in the process of arming to fight for independence from Spain. Churchill smoked between fourteen to sixteen cigars a day. He always chose the rich dark brown *maduros* (see Color) and preferred Double Coronas. The large Double Corona size* came to be so identified with this great statesman that a number of Cuban manufacturers, including Romeo y Julieta,* eventually named their Double Corona model* after Churchill. It has been calculated that Churchill smoked close to 250,000 cigars in his lifetime.

Winston Churchill, 1959.

levels and a light brushing off, they vanish without leaving any trace of damage behind. Of course, the wrapper's color and appearance has nothing to do with the cigar's flavor, which depends on the filler. The wrapper is no more than a thin outer layer, which provides a nuance of taste rather than its basis.

Churchill, Winston

Sir Winston Leonard Spencer Churchill (1874–1965), the English Prime Minister instrumental in the Allies' victory of World War II, is one of history's most famous Havana

This astronomical figure can perhaps be cut in half due to the fact that, for reasons of health as well as personal taste, Churchill never smoked more than half of each cigar. He is known to have stated that the end of a great Havana is no better than that of a two-bit drugstore cigar.

> *"I drink a good deal, sleep little, and smoke cigar after cigar. That is why I am in two hundred percent shape."*
>
> Winston Churchill

■ Cigarillo

Cigarillos are little cigars, only slightly longer than cigarettes. They are made of tobacco scraps, usually have no binder (see Composition), and have nothing to do with excellent single-region tobacco *puros* in terms of quality. Cigarillos are machine-made, and vastly inferior to cigars, but they account for ninety percent of cigar production. They are often smoked by cigar lovers who can't afford to invest the time or the money for the real thing. Cigarillos are sometimes favored by cigarette smokers for their comparative allure of unconventionality and novelty. Under certain circumstances and on the right occasion, they make an impressive fashion statement.

Cigarillos played a role in at least two revolutions.* They were smoked by early-twentieth-century Mexican insurgents, who used them to light bombs and dynamite. Cigarillos were also proudly puffed by Italians rebelling against Austrian rule in the mid-nineteenth century. The Italian soldiers flaunted their cigarillos in the presence of the Austrian foe, in defiance of laws which forbade smoking anything other that products of the Austro-Hungarian Empire.

■ Color

Tobacco leaf colors range from *clarissimo,* a pale green hue, to *oscuro,* which is almost black. A spectrum of some hundred shades separate these two extremes. The basic cigar colors include *claro claro,* a golden blonde, *claro,* a very light tan, *colorado claro,* or light brown, *colorado,* a reddish brown, *maduro colorado,* or brown, *maduro,* a rich dark brown, and the almost black *oscuro.*

Green *clarissimo* tobacco is produced by keeping the leaves out of the light, harvesting them early, and stabilizing their chlorophyll level by exposure to burning wood. *Claro claro* and *claro* leaves are harvested before they reach full maturity and quickly air-dried. *Colorado claro* leaves come from high up on the plant.* Exposed to sunlight and harvested late, *colorado claro* leaves are strong in flavor. *Colorado maduro* and *colorado* are quite similar. They are even higher on the plant than *colorado claro,* exposed to more direct sunlight, and harvested later. These fully developed leaves make for especially strong taste. *Maduro* leaves are from the top of the tobacco plant. They receive the most sun and are harvested late in the season to deliver the strongest flavor. *Oscuro* leaves come from the very tip of the plant and are the last of all to be harvested. Very few smokers enjoy their harsh, strong taste.

The wrapper is merely an outer layer and has little bearing on a cigar's flavor. Flavor

comes from the filler, which makes up the bulk of the cigar. If a black wrapper were to be filled with green tobacco, which never happens in reality, the result would be a light cigar.

Clarissimo is a favorite wrapper color for American aficionados.* In Europe, tastes run from *claro* to *maduro colorado,* with the lighter browns enjoying somewhat greater popularity. *Oscuros* are the closest thing to the "half-burning sticks" that Christopher Columbus and his sailors* were surprised to see in the natives' mouths when he happened upon the New World in 1492.

Eight cigar colors, from left to right: *Clarissimo, claro claro, claro, colorado claro, colorado, maduro colorado, maduro,* and *oscuro.*

■ Composition

From tip to tip, a cigar's physical features include the head, the body, and the foot; from the outside in, the wrapper, binder, and filler.

The head is the closed end placed in the smoker's mouth once it is cut in preparation for smoking. It is usually rounded; sometimes slightly pointy. The body is the entire length, whether cylindrical, straight, conical, or even twisted in shape. The foot is the cut open end of the cigar that shows the leaves.

The wrapper (also known as the *capa*, particularly when it is still in the form of a leaf) makes up the cigar's outer surface. It consists of a single, superior quality protective and highly resilient half-leaf, rolled in a spiral. The binder is composed of two half-leaves. These are superimposed and rolled in the opposite direction to the wrapper, which gives the cigar a degree of rigidity. The filler is comprised of up to three types of tobacco leaves whose combined qualities provide the cigar's specific attributes of strength, flavor, and aroma.

■ Cuba

Cuba is the Mecca of cigar production. It is the be-all and end-all to which all cigar-loving eyes are forever expectantly turned.

Spain, recognizing something worth fighting for, struggled for four hundred years to hold onto its monopoly on Cuban tobacco. Die-hard smugglers, pirates, and sea-faring entrepreneurs of all sorts followed suit. All these contradictory efforts had one final effect—to focus on and magnify the greatness of Cuban tobacco.

Up until the eighteenth century, the Spanish regarded their southern city of Seville* as the only place worthy of treating

Havana wrapper leaf.

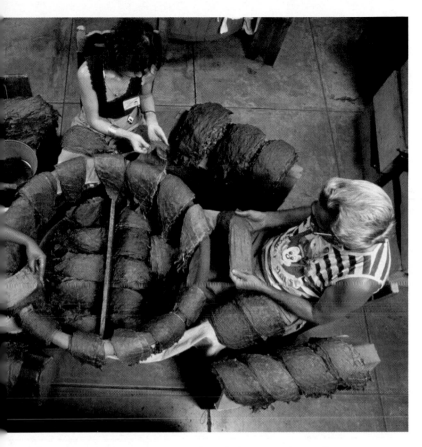

and processing the tobacco it imported from Cuba. This changed in 1717 with the accession to the throne of Philip V, who authorized the establishment of the first cigar factory in Havana. By 1740, King Philip had approved the founding of the first Cuban cigar company in Cuba. Cuban tobacco's popularity began to spread to England and North America by 1762, when British troops invaded Havana. In 1772 the Vuelta Abajo* region was first planted. It soon proved to be the best place in the world to grow cigar tobacco.

When Napoleon's troops invaded Spain in 1807, not long after the Seville factory had perfected the *puro,* the stock was looted. As a result, cigars spread as far as Moscow along with the invaders. Napoleon was defeated, but Havana* tobacco won the Western world.

In response to a growing worldwide demand, cigar factories multiplied in Cuba throughout the nineteenth century. *Tabaqueros** soon constituted an aristocracy of the people which cried out for independence, and won it in 1898. Cuban cigar production managed to develop and prosper during the many vicissitudes of the twentieth century. Nowadays, Cuba exports roughly 70 million cigars a year.

Tobacco leaf inspection in a Cuban cigar factory, 1992.

47

■ CUBAN BRANDS

The first known brand of cigar was registered in Havana by Bernardino Rencurrel in 1810. That same year Cabanas y Carbajol followed suit. Brand names were instituted in an effort to prevent counterfeiting and smuggling, and they soon became an effective mark of value and quality assurance as well. After Madrid's Cuban* tobacco monopoly ended in 1817 many tobacco companies appeared, and competition was fierce. By the middle of the nineteenth century most of the famous names now distributed by Habanos S.A. were in business. Partagas started in 1827, Por Larranaga in 1834, Punch in 1840, H. Upmann in 1844, El Rey del Mundo in 1848, and Romeo y Julieta* in 1850. Other important brands that were launched include Arturo Fuente, Bolivar, Cifuentes, Hoyo de Monterrey (see La Escepcion), Maria Guerrero, Rafael Gonzales, and Sancho Panza. While the names have more or less remained, ownership and control have changed over time. Cigar markets have always demonstrated great fluctuations and changes of fortune. Factories and brands have often been family owned, and as such subject to the interest level and capacities of inheritors, as well as to being purchased by larger concerns and the vicissitudes of fashion, history, and economic changes. While brands such as Antilla Cubana, La Imperiosa, Señora Cubana, and others simply removed themselves from the market quietly, Castro's arrival to power put an end to the vast majority before he changed his mind and reinstated a good number of brands (see Revolution and Production), recognizing their market value as representatives of Cuban heritage. The Henry Clay brand was of course suppressed, since this American politician was an ardent protectionist.

Two of the finest Cuban brands are of relatively recent creation. Montecristo,* whose No. 1 immediately took its place among the greats, was launched in 1935 by the Menendez brothers. And as the Cuban Revolution's representative brand of excellence, from its inception Cohiba was intended to be unequaled by any other cigar. While they do in fact have some rivals, Cohibas are always excellent.

49

■ CULTIVATION
Sun and Humidity

Tobacco seeds are planted in nurseries in mid-September by *vegueros* or plantation workers. The first plants are transferred outdoors two weeks later. Transplanting is in full swing by October, beginning with the *corojo* or wrapper plants, which take ninety days to mature. Next come the filler plants, called

Tobacco plants in a *caballeria* covered by *tapados,* Brazil.

criollo de sol, which reach maturity in only forty-five to seventy days. Good growth requires ample sun and humidity, but minimal rainfall. In the growth process, the leaves go from matte to shiny green and lose their down covering. During this time, plants are closely monitored in order to give appropriate care and to determine the exact harvesting time. Sixteen to seventeen leaves are picked from each plant, comprised of six tiers of two or three leaves. Tobacco flavor is strongest on the top tier, which receives the most sunlight, and weakest on the bottom.

The long harvesting season runs from early January to late March or early April. Leaves are picked one by one over the period, depending on their maturity. Wrapper plants yield sixteen quintals, or a hundredweight (1,808 pounds) per acre, or 40 quintals per hectare. Smaller in stature and in leaf size, filler plants yield only thirteen to fifteen quintals (1,492 to 1,672 pounds) per acre, or 33 to 37 quintals per hectare. Tobacco plantations are sectioned off into *caballerias,* areas measuring 33.4 acres (13.5 hectares). Some of the *caballerias* are covered by *tapados,* lengths of white cotton suspended by pickets to protect the growing plants from damage due to excessive sunlight, harsh wind, and parasites. Leaves from such protected plants are used for wrappers. Harvesting is immediately followed by a preliminary sorting that takes place in the *casa de tabaco*—specially ventilated wooden drying* huts in the fields. The dried leaves are stacked for the first natural fermentation* which occurs at under 104°F (40°C).

The drying and first fermenting stages take from twenty to sixty days. Then the leaves are ready to go to the *escogida,** a festival held when the leaves are chosen and graded.

▩ Dandy

Dandies were men who dressed with an elegance that was often sublime to the point of ridiculousness. They appeared throughout the Western world in the first half of the nineteenth century, and were especially prominent in England and France, which developed a sort of style rivalry in terms of the phenomenon. Aestheticism, urbane wit, and a privileging of artifice over nature generally went hand in hand with the dandy outlook on life.

The apogee of dandyism occurred in the person of George Bryan "Beau" Brummell (1778–1840). The Prince of Wales himself was known to regularly stop by Brummell's

Henri de Toulouse-Lautrec. *Monsieur Louis Pascal.* 1893. Musée Toulouse-Lautrec, Albi.

G. J. Hamilton. *Indian Holding Cigars*. 1865. Musée du Nouveau-Monde, La Rochelle, France.

house to be present for the crowning moments of his dressing routine, an affair which could take several hours. By the 1830s, the Havana cigar, along with Brummell's blue jackets and impeccable starched white neckwear, became an emblem of the dandies. The cigar symbolized the sort of ephemeral, cultural pleasure they so appreciated. The French writer Stendhal said of himself: "I write the way one smokes a cigar." Writer George Sand, among the first women to publicly flaunt a cigar, made her position quite clear by declaring that the cigar was the "perfect complement to an idle and elegant lifestyle."

Idle cigar-smoking also flourished in the "seegar divans," beginning around 1830. Ten years later every London club had such a room, furnished in the Oriental style, where fine spirits and cigars could be luxuriantly savored. Finally, there was the cigar-holder to consummate the union between dandy and cigar. Thanks to this chic accessory, often made of amber or meerschaum, dandies were able to protect their gloves and fingers from tobacco stains. With their cult-like celebration of life's transitory pleasures, these spiffy dressers were opposed to leaving messy reminders amid the dying embers.

Davidoff, Zino

Zino Davidoff (1906–1994) was the twentieth century's greatest cigar magnate. Cigars brought Davidoff a fortune, and he brought many innovations to cigars and the industry. He was an aficionado in every sense. "I owe everything to cigars," Davidoff wrote in his *Connoisseur's Book of the Cigar*. "They have given me moments of ecstasy and anxiety, moments of happiness while working or relaxing, and whatever knowledge and wisdom I have gained over the years, I also owe to cigars."

Born in Kiev in the Ukraine, Davidoff fled the pogroms with his family at the age of four. His father, a blender of Turkish tobacco, set up business in Geneva, Switzerland in 1911. When he turned twenty, Davidoff went on a long trip to Latin America to study cigars up close. He spent 1928–32 in Cuba,* where he learned the well-kept secrets* of fine cigar-making. Upon returning to Switzerland, he built Europe's first temperature-controlled humidor storeroom in the basement of his father's shop.

Davidoff's career took off during World War II, when he was approached by the Cuban authorities to store and sell the millions of cigars stockpiled in European free ports. Davidoff became "Mister Cigar," and the family shop at 2, rue de la Rive in Geneva became the aficionado's Mecca for Cuban cigars in Europe. After the war, Cuba once again turned to

Zino Davidoff.

Davidoff to revive interest in cigars, which had fallen off with war shortages. Davidoff's idea, which met with great success, was to launch his "Châteaux" line in 1947. Using cigars manufactured by Hoyo de Monterrey, Davidoff marketed this line of top-quality cigars named after famous French wines. The first was Châteaux Latour, to be followed by Margaux, Laffitte, Haut-Brion, and others, including the renowned Dom Pérignon. In 1968, Fidel Castro offered Davidoff the unique opportunity to make his own brand in Cuba. The next year, Davidoff's Cuban-made No. 1 and No. 2 appeared (see Number), followed by the 1000, 2000, 3000, 4000, and 5000. These cigars were all immediate successes. Next Davidoff started the Zino line in Honduras* to cater to the American market. This annoyed the Cuban government and, along with a range of other complications, led to Davidoff's break with Cuba in 1989. Today nineteen Davidoff brand models* are produced in the Dominican Republic,* while twelve others are made in Honduras under the Zino name. The Zino trademark is also used for Davidoff cigars from Sumatra and Brazil.* Today, Davidoff is owned by Oettinger, a distinguished tobacco company in Basel, Switzerland.

■ Discovery

When Christopher Columbus landed in Cuba* in the fall of 1492, he sent two crew members ashore, Rodrigo de Jerez and Luis de Torres. They described the "great number of Indians, men and women, walking around with a little lighted stick

Cigar manufacturer in Cibao, Dominican Republic, 1991.

made from a kind of plant whose aroma it was their custom to inhale." This is the first mention of the cigar in history.

The Cubans were not the only Native Americans to smoke. The custom was widespread throughout the Caribbean, Mexico, Central America, Columbia, Venezuela, and Brazil.* Bartoloméo de Las Casas, a member of the expedition, reported: "The natives wrap the dried herbs in a certain leaf, in the manner of a musket formed of paper. . . and having lighted one end of it, by the other they suck, absorb, or receive that smoke inside with their breath . . . they call these muskets *tabacos*."

According to Cuban historians—as noted by Vincente Pinzon in a ship's log from Columbus's exploratory expedition—Rodriguo de Jerez was the first European to smoke a cigar every day, starting on 28 October 1492. For that reason, Jerez is still a national hero in modern Cuba.

■ Dominican Republic

Cigar-making took off on Hispaniola Island after the fall of the Batista regime (see Revolution) in Cuba. Growers who fled Castro's Cuba sought to recreate the success of Cuba's premier tobacco growing region, Vuelta Abajo*, in the northeastern Dominican Republic's Vega Real where the climate and the humidity* levels are nearly identical. The American embargo on Cuban products was a boon to their largely successful efforts. Soon many of the larger concerns, which had been growing tobacco in the Canary Islands, Jamaica, and Puerto Rico, were attracted to the Dominican Republic as well.

Many experts consider the Dominican tobacco labor force to be the best in the world, and some aficionados* find Dominican cigars at least the equal of their Cuban counterparts. In fact many of the world's better cigars are now crafted in the

Dominican Republic, including both those made from tobacco grown locally and those comprised of interesting blends. As far as the tobacco itself is concerned, in addition to an admirable lighter native Dominican variety of tobacco plant, Olor Dominicano, the expatriate Cuban growers began primarily cultivating new varieties, most notably Piloto Cubano. This is a superb, particularly aromatic tobacco that derives from Cuban seeds. Dominican tobacco is renowned the world over for the excellence of its filler and binder leaves (see Composition).

■ Draw

A cigar's draw depends upon how tightly it has been rolled, its humidity, and its ring gauge (or diameter). If it is too tight,

a cigar will not draw. If it is too dry, it will burn* faster than it can be consumed. Too easy a draw is called "hot" and a cigar that is too tight is called "plugged." Thickness is a major factor in the ease and consistency in lighting.* Larger diameter cigars have better draws than narrower cigars. You barely have to inhale, they burn consistently and they rarely go out. A good cigar that has been well pierced or lanced and correctly lit, will stay burning and ready for the smoker to draw at will. The smoker should never have to draw on the cigar to keep it lit. A cigarillo* requires more attention than a double corona. Neophytes should start with larger cigars—despite the risk that they will like them so much that an interest in small cigars may never develop.

Vista (detail), c. 1860, England. Bibliothèque des Arts décoratifs, Paris.

Inside a tobacco drying shed, France.

Drying

The drying of tobacco leaves begins immediately after they are picked, when they are brought to a *casa de tabaco* (drying shed) to reduce their moisture content. Leaves are tied by their stems in twos with cotton thread, and hung from horizontal wooden rods. Drying lasts between twenty days and three months, depending on whether the leaf is filler, binder, or wrapper (see Composition). Strong and mild tobaccos are not dried in the same manner. And the term "drying" itself is almost a misnomer. Ripening might be better. In any event, this ripening or air curing process causes a reduction of volume and weight, at the same time that

the tobacco aromas concentrate in the leaf. They must not dry out completely, however. A completely dry leaf is a dead leaf. The goal is for the leaves to become thinner while remaining flexible and oily. *Vegueros* (planters) keep a constant watch over them. If the sun beating down on the palm branch roof is too intense, the ground is dampened. If it rains too much, a fire is lit. Drying takes place through air circulation. In Cuba,* doorways on the east and west sides are always left open as are air circulation slats beneath the roof. If dehumidification is taking too long the leaves are placed outside for a "sun bath." Sometimes heat is used to stabilize chlorophyll content, which enables the leaves to remain green.

Following page: Wrapper leaf selection during drying, Cuba.

Alfred Dunhill rose to fame for his expert pipe tobacco blends, and for his pipes themselves. The latter can always be recognized by their little white dot and are considered incomparable. Dunhill's *The Gentle Art of Smoking* continues to be an important reference for anyone interested in the topic. Along with Zino Davidoff,* Dunhill was offered the honor of making his own cigars in Cuba* in 1968. The eight resulting cigar models* bore the Dunhill label up until 1992. The greatest among them is arguably the Havana Club, an outstanding double corona (see Size) similar to the renowned Montecristo* A, and sold in individual boxes. Today Dunhill makes twelve models in the Dominican Republic,* five in the Canary Islands, and three in Holland.

Alfred Dunhill shop, London, 1907.

Dunhill, Alfred

The name Alfred Dunhill has been synonymous with English tobacco since the nineteenth century. Dunhill had the ingenious idea of setting up an enormous walk-in humidor at his store on 30 Duke Street in London. Preferred clients can have their cigars "looked after" by the Dunhill staff of experts, or rent maturing compartments on a yearly basis for their favorite cigars. Winston Churchill is known to have had several of these "keepers," filled with thousands of precious cigars. At the start of World War II, he had them moved to a deep cellar, which allowed them to escape damage during the Blitz, when German bombs leveled the Dunhill building.

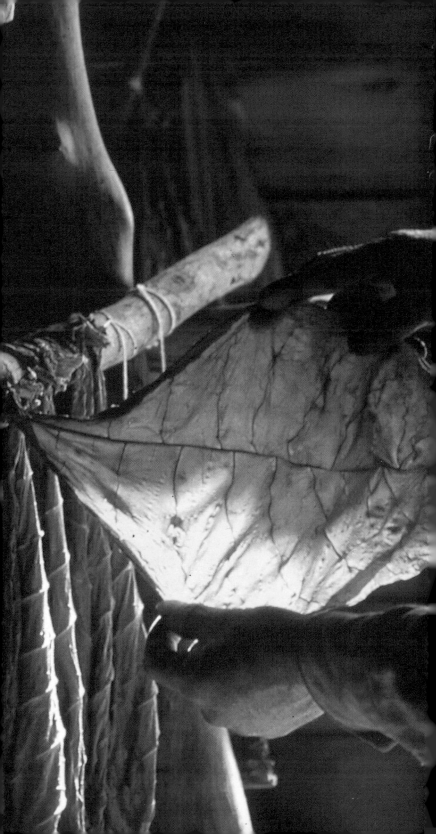

■ DUTCH CIGARS

The Dutch were a major commercial and colonizing power in the sixteenth century, especially in Southeast Asia,* when they began trading in tobacco. After establishing themselves as one of Europe's major pipe-smoking countries (as seventeenth-century paintings amply illustrate) towards the end of the eighteenth century, Holland joined Spain and Portugal as a leader in the manufacture* of cigars. Today, in terms of population, the Dutch are the number one producer of cigars and cigarillos.*

So what kind of cigars do the Dutch produce? Their major suppliers are still former colonies in the Indonesian and Malay archipelagos: Java, Sumatra, and Borneo. These islands produce high quality tobaccos that are darker, stronger, and less smooth than Caribbean tobaccos. In Sumatra, the superior tobacco-growing area is Medan, on the northwest coast of the island. In Java, the tobacco grown in the Vorstenlanden and Besoeki sections are the best. Tobacco from Havana* has been cultivated around Medan, in the Deli province, since the nineteenth century. These plants, originally of Peruvian stock, which have been acclimatized to Cuba* for centuries, yield smooth, pliant leaves with very fine grains. They are excellent wrappers. Other tobaccos grown in the region are light, clear, and blonder. They are mild with a slight bitterness upon lighting.*

Cigars have been produced in Indonesia and Myanmar for four centuries. These very dry, mild, light, and easy-to-smoke cigars, go under the appellation "Dutch," and are mainly distributed to the world by dealers in Amsterdam and Rotterdam. Their taste is more or less the standard in Northern Europe—to such an extent that German cigars have for a long time imitated them and Havana tobacco is rarer in Northern than in Southern Europe.

◼ ESCOGIDA
A Celebration of Selection

The *escogida* is a festival held after the leaves have undergone drying and initial fermentation.* The festivities revolve around the selection of leaves made by buyers from Cubatabaco, the government agency that replaced private specialists after the Cuban Revolution. The *escogida* corresponds to traditional celebrations held at harvest time throughout the world. Planters make their leaves look their best, re-humidifying them with a solution of tobacco, water, and secret* ingredients. Each plantation has its own jealously guarded formula for this solution which triggers the second fermentation* of the leaves. Sheaves of leaves are proudly displayed in decorated palm leaf wrappers, and bundles called *tercios* are sent off to the factories. Each *tercio* is marked with a number indicating place of origin. As for quality-control measures, the expert buyers select leaves and class them according to several dozen categories. Determining factors include size, color,* weight, shape, texture, pliability, fermentation quality, thickness, and vein size. Ultimately decisions depend on the experts' experience, talent, and intuition. They bestow prizes on the best of the leaves from each harvest.

Natives Smoking Tobacco. Engraving from André Thevet's *Cosmographie universelle.* 1575.

◼ Etymology

It took over three centuries for the word "cigar" to finally catch on. For a long time there was no agreement over what to call the various shapes and sizes of smoking "tobacco rolls" or "tobacco sticks." In Cuba,* cigars have almost always and continue to be referred to as *tabacos.* It was formerly thought that the word cigar came from the Spanish word *cigaral* (cicada), alluding to the insect's shape and skin. Today experts agree that the term is derived from an ancient Mayan word. According to the expert Gunther Stahl, the word *Jiq* or *Ciq,* is found in the *Popol Vuh,* a chronicle of the Mayan Quiché tribe, where it meant cigar. The Spanish *cigarollo* derives from the Mayan *Ciq-Sigan.* The term *Cigale* is used in the writings of Father Labat, a Dominican missionary

First fermentation of tobacco leaves, Cuba.

in the West Indies (c. 1700). *Seegar* is an entry in the *New English Dictionary,* published in 1735. Not long after, *cigar* and *cigarro* could be heard. But confusion and indecision over the cigar's nomenclature reigned well into the nineteenth century, as seen in the London "seegar divans" (see Dandy).

■ Fermentation

Tobacco leaves can remain fresh for years as long as they are kept humid, and this, like many of tobacco's other characteristics, is a result of fermentation itself. Tobacco leaves are fermented three times during the cigar-making process. The first fermentation takes place on the plantation after drying* in the racks of the *casa de tabaco.* Drying and the initial fermentation take between twenty and sixty days. The second fermentation is part of the conditioning process they undergo for the *escogida** festival, before being sent to factories. Filler tobacco is fermented at this stage in *tercios* (sheaves); wrapper tobacco in wooden barrels (see Composition). The third fermentation happens in the factory before blending,* and usually takes between one and three years, though it can last as long as a decade for truly great tobacco. The process requires a high level of precision and constant monitoring. It is performed by highly trained and talented experts. The sheaves are intermittently unbound and the barrels emptied; the leaves are then aired out, re-hydrated, and repositioned. The longer

63

Finca in the Vinales valley, Cuba.

the third fermentation, the better the resulting tobacco. As the process advances, the tobacco's aroma gradually becomes more concentrated and gains in complexity. Finished cigars are stocked in warehouses to stabilize their humidity. This takes place the summer after fabrication, following yet another period of fermentation.

■ Finca

A *finca* is a Cuban farm. A *finca de tabac* grows tobacco. The smallest *fincas* can be less than fifteen acres (5 hectares), while the larger ones, which became State farms following the Revolution,* can be up to several hundred acres. A few of the very biggest *fincas* extend to 2,500 acres (1,000 hectares). All Cuban tobacco-growing

fincas, large or small, produce their own seed from plants* which are specially set aside and allowed to flower until the seeds have germinated, forty days after planting. Each finca also has its own nursery where the seeds are sown. Once they reach about six inches (15 cm) in height, they are transplanted to fields. The harvest takes place between forty-five and ninety days later, depending on whether the leaves are wrapper or filler tobacco (see Composition). Wrapper leaves take up to twice as long as fillers to mature. As they mature, leaves are individually picked and immediately taken to the casa de tabaco, a drying* hut full of palm wood racks with an east-west orientation that allows the hut's sides to be lit by sunlight only in the morning and

evening. Air comes in through the permanently open doors on either end, and goes out through slats under the roof.

Fine Food

While cigars are certainly not comestible, nor to be smoked while eating, they still belong to the world of wining, dining, and gourmet delights. Progressive culinary advances and innovations greatly improved dining options in a number of American and English cities— New York and London foremost among them—throughout the 1990s and into the twenty-first century. A more developed appreciation of cigar smoking, on the part of chefs, wine stewards, and diners alike, went hand in hand with these advances. These days many top restaurants sell cigars along

Jean Béraud (1839–1936). *Dinner at the Ambassadeurs Restaurant.* Musée Carnavalet, Paris.

with after-dinner drinks. Some have even installed sumptuous smoking rooms especially for this purpose.

An after-dinner cigar must be chosen to complement the meal that preceded it. A meal of shellfish cannot end in the same way as one where the main dish was wild boar, for example. The flavor of a fine Havana (see Principles of Enjoyment) is heightened by the after-effects of a particular entrée eaten less than an hour before and still subtly lingering on one's palate. When carefully chosen, following expert advice if needed and available, the right cigar is certainly the perfect end to a wonderful meal.

First Reported Smokers

During Christopher Columbus' famous first voyage in search of "the Indies," he set anchor off Cuba and sent Rodrigo de Jerez and Luis de Torres inland to explore the island. They were the first to have recounted seeing the indigenous people smoke tobacco leaves. Jerez became a consummate smoker, and was probably the first person to smoke outside of the New World. Back in Spain, he was condemned by the Inquisition when he was seen exhaling smoke. The first report of North American tobacco comes from the explorer Jacques Cartier, who encountered smokers in Montreal in 1535.

André Thevet accompanied Nicolas Durand de Villeganon on his expedition to Brazil* in the 1550s. Thevet wrote what became standard and sometimes fantastical accounts of the "cannibals of Brazil" as well as descriptions of the Brazilians' therapeutic use of the plant, which he cultivated, smoked, and recommended to others upon his return to France. At the same time the Frenchman Jean Nicot was sent to Lisbon to negotiate the marriage of the French and Portuguese heirs to their respective thrones. This effort failed but Nicot encountered the plant whose scientific name (*Nicotiana Tabacum*) and whose chief active principle (the alkoloid nicotine) now bear his name. "I am amazed by its practical properties" he wrote in 1560, sending sample plants back to France. Nicot recommended tobacco to the queen of France, Catherine de' Medici, as a remedy for her migraines. When the cure worked tobacco became all the rage. Tobacco was apparently introduced to the English some five years later by Sir John Hawkins, but remained mainly an indulgence of English sailors* for the next few decades.

André Thevet (1503–1592), *Self-portrait.* Engraving. Bibliothèque national de France, Paris.

Gérard Père et Fils

In recent years, Gérard Père et Fils has joined the ranks of Dunhill and Davidoff, emerging as a power to reckon with in the forefront of worldwide Havana trade. Based in Geneva, both father and son, as well as mother and daughter, are consummate cigar connoisseurs. The Gérard family knows Havana tobacco inside out, from seed to box seal. Their flagship store, located in the Noga Hilton Hotel in Geneva, is a spacious shrine to the *puro* constructed from Cuban cedar, the wood used to make Havana cigar boxes.*

Gérard Père et Fils brings state-of-the-art technology to bear on their meticulous cigar handling and maturing. This special care gives their cigars an extra something in terms of flavor and freshness. Each box that arrives from Havana is opened and thoroughly inspected before it is put on sale, and constantly checked for the duration of its life in the shop. Every cigar is tested to monitor its maturity, and sold only at its peak. Their standards are so unrelentingly high that—although very infrequently—boxes have been shipped back to Havana due to inferior leaf quality.

The Cuban authorities are willing to put up with Gérard Père et Fils' exacting demands, firstly because their cigars are thoroughly up to snuff, and secondly because Gérard is the Havana cigar's main spokesperson to the world today. The Gérards sell and swear by Havanas only. They go to Cuba each year during the harvest, and participate in selecting and blending* the leaves for the choice cigar models sold without rings* under the name Sélection Gérard.

Gérard Père et Fils have popularized short, fat cigars with perfect draw,* such as the Partagas D4 model and Hoya de Monterrey's Epicures. They were awarded Cubatabaco's twenty-fifth anniversary medal and accorded the great honor of being authorized to display the Cubatabaco logo in their shop.

Gérard Fils.

■ HAVANA TOBACCO

The sun and the climate on the island of Cuba* are ideal for tobacco growing—a fact that has been widely accepted since the Elizabethan era. The greatest among Cuba's four incomparable growing regions is Vuelta Abajo.*

Cigars grown and crafted with the utmost skill by experts exiled from Castro's Cuba, under the similar geographical and climatic conditions of nearby Honduras* and the Dominican Republic,* and using Cuban seeds and sometimes even soil brought from Cuba, have never quite made the mark. Countless well-planned, agriculturally sound, ingenious attempts have been made, will continue to be made, and will most likely fail every time. This is because the special nature of Havana cigars transcends logic.

What makes the Havana truly superior is the staying-power of its indescribable aroma and flavor.* This long-lasting taste cannot be rivaled by even the strongest of non-Cuban cigars, produced with the black tobacco of Brazil,* for instance. However earthy or woodsy it may be, a Havana always leaves the smoker with an impression of smoothness associated with calm and satisfaction.

John Bachmann.
Birdseye View of Havana.
Nineteenth century. Engraving. Museo de las Américas, Madrid.

◼ Havana History

From a historical perspective, the expansion of the cigar industry in Havana coincided with its decline in Seville.* It was in this Andalusian city, that the *puro* was perfected with its separate wrapper, binder, and filler parts (see Composition) at the end of the eighteenth century. The *puro* is made only of tobacco leaves. Previously, cigar wrapper layers were made with non-tobacco leaves. With the advent of the *puro* came the special growing, drying,* and fermentation* techniques suited to produce wrapper tobacco leaves.

In the early nineteenth century, the Napoleonic Wars and the English maritime blockade cut Spain off from Cuba.* Seville had only its reserves to fall back on, and these were soon looted by French soldiers, who spread a taste for cigars throughout Europe, wherever their invading army went. Back in Havana, the Cubans were left to cultivate their tobacco crops on their own. The first Cuban brands appeared in Havana in 1810. Once the fighting was over, naval transport began to improve vastly with the introduction of steamships, and trade with Europe continued to expand. Seville could no longer compete with its former supplier, and Spain granted Cuba rights for growing and selling tobacco in 1817. By 1863, there were 516 Havana

disease. Fortunately, cigar smokers are less prone to these diseases than other smokers. This is due to the slowness of cigar smoking—which is markedly different, for instance, from chain-smoking cigarettes. Cigar tobacco is so strong that it is immediately satisfying. And not inhaling the smoke helps keep the trachea and lungs clear of some danger. Fully inhaling masochists are few and far between. Che Guevera was one (see Revolution), but he apparently did so to try to calm the asthma that plagued him throughout his life.

In fact, Caribbean tobaccos have lower levels of nicotine than most other varieties, as any Cuban will quickly tell you—given the chance. Cost (see Price) is another impediment to abusive cigar use. While cigars are not completely risk-free, they are certainly the least dangerous smoke around.

William Bradley. Tobacco detoxification poster, late nineteenth century. Bibliothèque des Arts décoratifs, Paris.

cigar factories which employed 15,128 workers. This figure does not include the numerous prisoners put to cigar-making tasks in the four local jails.

■ Health

Warnings like those of the American Surgeon General appear on tobacco products in many countries. But from the fifteenth to the seventeenth century, tobacco was considered to be a great curative medication, rather than a product that causes cancer and heart disease. The toxicity of nicotine ($C_{10}H_{14}N_2$) has been known for more than a century, as have the heavy smoker's risk of developing cancer (particularly of the lung and throat) and cardiovascular

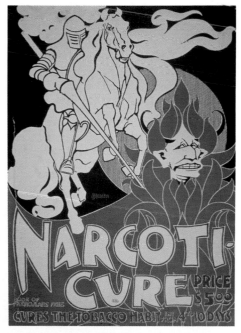

Cigar boxes designed by David Linley for Dunhill.

■ Home Storage

Proper cigar storage is of primary importance. Like fine wine and liquor (see Alcohol) cigars evolve in aging. When they are two or three years old, cigars give off a little oil at the same period of the year that tobacco plants in their native land begin to blossom. Havana *puros* are made three to four years after the tobacco is harvested. They can be safely stored for fifteen years in the dark, with a relative humidity* level of between sixty and seventy percent, and a temperature kept stable at 59 to 68°F (15 to 20°C). Exposure to sun or artificial light discolors and dries out cigars. The leaves become brittle and their aroma progressively sours. Cold will also make cigars dry, so they should never be put in a refrigerator. The best storage conditions simulate the Caribbean climate, where cigars stay perfectly fresh. A variety of cigar storage options are available for maintaining the right humidity and temperature. Davidoff* sells excellent self-regulating cases. Other simpler and less expensive systems come equipped with sponges, a thermometer, and humidity meter. They work well when correctly monitored. These cigar humidifiers, called humidors, range in size from single-cigar cases to cabinets and walk-in room-sized models for commercial use. Placed in a well-functioning humidor, a cigar that is dehydrated, without, however, having completely dried out, can be reconditioned in a matter of weeks.

■ Honduras

In 1977, the great cigar expert Zino Davidoff* chose the Central American country of Honduras as the spot to try and develop top-drawer non-Cuban *puros*. Up until then, Honduras had no reputation for cigar making beyond its borders. Davidoff set up in

Santa Rosa de Copan, in a factory dating from 1785, the last in the country to still maintain its own plantations. The Mayas had grown tobacco in the Copan province for centuries. Here, Davidoff launched the Zino line, with the Zino Corona Extra, the Zino Long Corona, and the Zino Mouton Cadet I and II models. Some American aficionados* today consider the Honduran Hoyo de Monterrey Excalibur to be the world's finest cigar. The American Rothman Company and Dunhill* of England also make cigars in Honduras. Honduran cigars are aromatic and mild. They are best suited to American cigar tastes, and for this reason are most successful in the United States.

From left to right: Pride of Jamaica, Santa Clara (Mexico), Fundadores (Jamaica), Don Pepe (Mexico), Hoyo de Monterrey Excalibur (Honduras), Mocambo (Mexico), Chivis (Honduras), Steed (Jamaica), and Mocha (Honduras).

73

Humidor.

■ Humidity

Tobacco's arch enemies are wind and rain. The less it rains throughout the year, the happier the plantation directors are. The dread of too much rain is apparent in the first extant Cuban piece of writing on the topic of tobacco, which dates from the seventeenth century. A letter from the planter Demetrio Pela, originally from the Canary Islands in Spain, credits his Native American partner Erioxil Panduca with saying, "The gods have decreed that tobacco only needs water twice a month. Too much water steals away its honey."

High humidity levels of between seventy and eighty percent are nevertheless crucial for the tobacco plant's proper growth. After harvesting, the tobacco must be scrupulously stored and handled to maintain proper humidity levels at all times.

■ Image

The image of the authentic cigar, unlike the cigarillo,* is not particularly positive. Cigars are often automatically associated with ideas of selfish wealth and insensitive arrogance. Yet even though cigars first caught on in Europe among the idle rich, including dandies,* throughout the Western world they have been consistently smoked by people from all walks of life. In fact, foot soldiers were responsible for spreading the cigar throughout Europe during the Napoleonic Wars. Later, the image of American GIs manning their tanks with black cigarillos sticking out of the corners of their mouths greatly helped to revive an interest in cigars

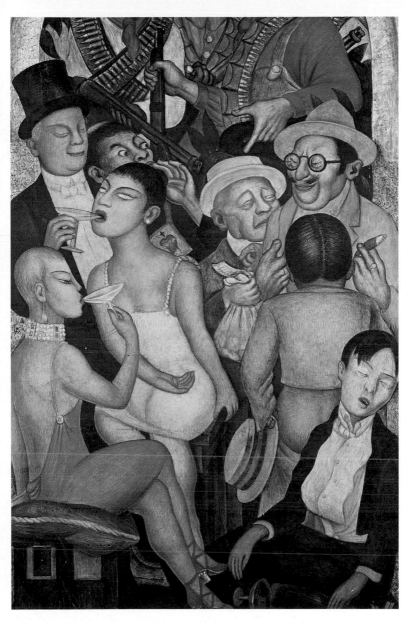

among the Allies at the end of World War II. It should be remembered that, like corn and other new food staples, tobacco formed a link between the colonizers of the New World and the original inhabitants. An enjoyment of fine cigars is something that could certainly spark a conversation and even strike up a friendship between an English Member of Parliament and a Cuban field worker. Not all cigars are expensive, and among the many thousands of cigars available to choose from, there is one to fit every taste and budget. Multinational capitalism may indeed have grave consequences, but capitalists have no monopoly on cigar smoking.

Diego Rivera, *The Orgy* (detail). 1923–1928. Fresco. Ministry of Education, Mexico.

Italy

A small quantity of tobacco is cultivated in Italy, in Tuscany. The very dark, bitter yield is used to make Toscani cigars, renowned for their pungency and strength. These rough-looking cigars bear picturesque large rings* around their midsection, decorated with the red, white and green colors of the Italian flag.

Italians are generally not Havana fans, though appreciation for Cuban tobacco may be on the rise, especially in northern Italy. Suppliers of Cuban and other imported cigars are relatively rare, so many Italian aficionados* turn to Switzerland for their stock.

La Escepcion

La Escepcion is one of the very greatest Havana brands. It was created by José Gener, who was born near Barcelona in Spain's Catalonia region. In the early nineteenth century, Catalan merchants were active European importers of Cuban tobacco.

Gener went to Cuba in 1831, at the age of thirteen, on the advice of his uncle, Miguel Jané y Gener, who made Majagua cigars, a low-quality brand, in the Pinar del Rio province. In 1851, José Gener opened a tobacco shop in Havana, and, once again at his uncle's suggestion, decided to develop his own cigar. He registered the brand name, La Escepcion, with a misspelling, but when informed of his error, the proud Gener opted to keep it. La Escepcion was a huge hit abroad, especially in the United States.* The prestige model* was the Regalias, which had a cylindrical body and a pointed head.

Even before creating La Escepcion, Gener had bought Hoyo de Monterrey, and in the end gave priority to that brand. Gener raised the Hoyo de Monterrey brand to the highest degree of quality —to the point of eclipsing La Escepcion, which remains one of the marvels of Cuba.

Toscani cigars, Italy.

him remedy;
For she of hearties had great intendiment,
Taught of the Nymphe which from her infancy
Her nourced had in trew nobility:
There, whether yet divine Tobacco were,
Or Panachea, or Polygony,
She fownd, and brought it to her patient deare
Who al this while lay bleeding out his hart-blood scare."

Havana cigar club in Paris.
Photograph by Léonard Freed.

Paul Verlaine.
Self-portrait as a dandy.
1889–1890.

■ Lighting

Lighting up is a key moment in in cigar smoking. Fine cigars are specially rolled* so that the draw* is as consistent and effortless as possible. But even the best cigar will present problems if improperly lit. To help ensure that the tobacco burns* at an even rate as the cigar is smoked,* the whole foot (end) of the cigar should be lit in several quick puffs. The first puffs are never the best, since a cigar needs to heat up from smoking to release its full flavor. The flame used to light a cigar should be strong and odorless. For this reason, sulfur-tipped matches and fuel lighters should be avoided.

In the past, there was a prejudice against letting a cigar go out and re-lighting. This practice is no longer taboo, and smokers can pause and re-light as they please.

■ Literature

The earliest mention of tobacco in English literature is in Edmund Spenser's *Fairie Queen,* in 1590. In Book III, Canto VI, 32 of the epic poem, Belphoebe includes tobacco with other medicinal herbs she gathered to heal Timais:

"Into the woods thenceforth in haste she went,
To seeke for hearties that mote

In Spenser's time, tobacco was considered something of an experimental dietary supplement whose miraculous healing possibilities had yet to be entirely revealed. By the nineteenth century, when the virtues of cigars had been thoroughly discovered and documented, the cigar found a great spokesman in Rudyard Kipling, author of *The Jungle Book.* It is in his poem *The Betrothed* that Kipling notoriously wrote: "A woman is just a woman, but a good cigar is a smoke." This line may have provided inspiration for the slew of misogynistic remarks that have given cigars a bad reputation. Appealing one-liners can be culled from Mark Twain, the nineteenth-century literary wit of America. A native of Connecticut's tobacco-growing region, Twain was a staunchly devoted aficionado,* one of history's greatest. "I smoke in moderation—only one cigar at a time," quipped Twain. "Eating and sleeping," he maintained, "are the only activities that should be allowed to interrupt a man's enjoyment of his cigar." Exceptionally tenacious by nature, Twain would not part with his cigar-smoking, even when destitute. "If smoking cigars is not permitted in heaven, I won't go," Twain insisted.

Sublime tobacco! which from east to west
Cheers the tar's labour or the Turkoman's rest;
Which on the Moslem's ottoman two divides
His hours, and rivals opium and his brides;
Magnificent in Stamboul, but less grand,
Though not less loved in Wapping or the Strand;
Divine in hookahs, glorious in a pipe,
When tipped with amber, mellow, rich and ripe:
Like other charmers, wooing the caress,
More dazzlingly when daring in full dress,
Yet thy true lovers more admire by far
Thy naked beauties—hand me a cigar!

Lord Byron, from "The Island," 1823

■ Manila

Cigars from the Philippines, known as Manila cigars, were amazingly popular in the nineteenth century. People even preferred them over Havana cigars. As the cigar expert Eugene Marsan put it in 1929, "When you cannot get hold of a Manila, you can console yourself with a Havana cigar. It is not demeaning, but it is a compromise." Spain planted tobacco in the Philippines in the sixteenth century. Nowadays, the best Philippine tobacco is grown in the Cagayan River valley, on the island of Luzon. The leaves are light brown, thin, not very strong, and bitter. They are best blended* with tobacco from Brazil.* Their present qualities and former glory lead one to conclude that either tastes changed radically or former know-how disappeared over time. There are two main brands, Flor de la Isabella, and the rarely exported Alhambra. In smoking, better models* actually begin well but finish poorly. Flor de Isabella's strong and harsh Elephant's foot model, with its easily recognizable rectangular foot and small round head, is probably the best known.

■ Manufacture Begins Internationally

The first European tobacco factories were established in Spain in the seventeenth century. At first they produced snuff rather than cigars. Cigars (as differentiated from what was smoked in the New World during the Age of Discovery,*) were invented in Seville,* which began producing them in 1676. The famous impressive buildings of the royal tobacco manufactory (which

now house the University of Andalucia) were built in 1731 by King Ferdinand IV.

Holland, using what it cultivated on the Islands of Sumatra and Java, as well as other of its West Indian and southeast Asian* colonies, opened its first tobacco works at the same time as Spain. French cigars did not appear

until 1740, with the first factories in Brittany (see Altadis), and the Vatican authorized the painter Peter Vendler to open Italy's first tobacco factory in Rome in 1779. The first German factory opened in 1790. 1810 was a major year in the history of cigar manufacturing. The first American tobacco works were set up in and around Hartford, Connecticut (see United States), as Cuban factories began to multiply after the end of the Spanish monopoly. This was when Seville's golden age of tobacco, including its exclusive output of higher quality *puros* came to an end. The tobacco factories of Seville halted production definitively in 1900.

Leonard Defrance (1735–1805). *Visit to a Tobacco Factory.* Museum of Wallon Art, Liège.

■ MODELS

A cigar's model indicates how a cigar looks, its format, its physical characteristics, its exterior characteristics, shape, length and weight—but not its color* which has a separate classification system. Model is often synonymous with size. There are more than 950 cigar shapes inscribed within the official rolls of Havana's cigar manufacture board, with sizes ranging from *microscopicos* to *immensas*. Typical cigar size ranges between 2¾ to 8 inches (7 to 20 cm), that is, from half coronas to double coronas or magnums. Diameter ranges from a third to three quarters of an inch (10 to 20 mm).

A cigar's effect depends on the ratio between length and ring gauge, as well as composition.* The filler is essential. You can see it, and to some extent check its quality at the foot of a cigar. The nature of a cigar's draw is largely a factor of its diameter, or ring* gauge (RG). Larger diameters draw more easily, burn more slowly without getting too hot, and the smoke* is less likely to become bitter or acrid. Larger models do not necessarily produce stronger smokes, but they will fill the mouth more fully and evenly. This enables greater appreciation of the blending* of filler, binder, and wrapper.

Montecristo
Boxes, Cuba.

■ Montecristo

The hero of Alexander Dumas' *The Count of Monte-Cristo* (published in 1844) was certainly no stranger to cigars, and the success of the book, then as now, kept the name Monte Cristo in the air. But according to a member of the Menendez family, which founded the brand, Doña Dina Menendez Bastiony, the brand name is more the result of a happy coincidence than a conscious choice. One day in 1935 the family was sitting at a table in a Havana café, apparently just before embarking on a trip to Mount Burbona, in Altube, Spain. Their plans for launching a new brand of premium cigars were already underway, but they hadn't yet decided upon a name. They ordered a bottle of fine Italian wine, Lacryma-Christi—and it clicked. *Monte* Altube plus Lacryma-*Christi* led to Montecristo.

Another story is that in a Cuban factory, where a man was paid to read aloud to amuse the workers, the employees so enjoyed the novel that they wrote to Alexandre Dumas to ask for his blessing to name a cigar after his hero.

Movies

Cigar smoking has been seen on the silver screen ever since the birth of the seventh art. The earliest movie to feature cigar smoking was Georges Méliès' *Every Man His Own Cigar Lighter,* made in 1904. Ever since, countless film plots have revolved around cigar-smoking characters, from gangsters to bankers. In 1922, audiences were scandalized by Mae Busch, who portrayed "Princess" Olga Petschnikoff in Erich von Stroheim's masterpiece *Foolish Wives.* The character, a licentious grifter, betrayed her true colors in lighting up with gusto. Another high point in women's cigar smoking on celluloid comes in Orson Welles' 1958 *Touch of Evil,* where Marlene Dietrich makes a stunning appearance as a cigar-smoking Mexican madame in semi-retirement. Her reputation for cigar smoking, justified or not, is part of the Dietrich mystique.

Orson Welles himself was among the twentieth century's most inveterate and famous aficionados,* rivaling Fidel Castro (see Revolution) and Winston Churchill.* Welles, who frequently acted in his own films, often portrayed cigar-smoking protagonists, notably in *Citizen Kane.* As exemplified in this movie based on the true story of a newspaper magnate, cigar smoking symbolizes power, wealth, blind arrogance, and the nasty capitalist in general. Charlie Chaplin cemented this image with his many portraits

of filthy rich aficionados. In the final scene of *The Gold Rush,* the destitute Chaplain tramp chews an evil millionaire's cigar butt. An unlit cigar ever dangling from his mouth, Groucho Marx turns this convention on its head in his hilarious comedies.

Whether behind the scenes like Alfred Hitchcock or Stanley Kubrick, or in the public eye, like George Burns, Bill Cosby, Michael Douglas, Demi Moore, or Arnold Schwarzenegger, many film and television personalities have been known to relish a fine smoke. 1990s advertising campaigns, sponsored by tobacco companies anxious to play down the "bad guy" image associated with cigars, sought to take advantage of this fact by featuring contemporary cigar-loving movie stars.

Alfred Hitchcock during the filming of *The Birds,* 1962.

Orson Welles.

■ Number

Some brands classify their cigars by number. The most well known are those of Montecristo* and Davidoff.* While they are not mere inventions out of the blue, how the maker comes up with a certain number is not particularly clear. A Montecristo 1 is seven inches (18 cm) long with a diameter of ⅔ of an inch (17 mm) and a Montecristo 2 measures six inches (15.5 cm) with a diameter of ¾ of an inch (20 mm). Their largest cigar is the Montecristo A. This shift from numbers to letters is as logical as Romeo y Julieta's* Exhibition No. 4 and Cedros de Luxe 1, or Davidoff's* 2000, 4000, 2, and Chateaux line. Some people consider this a sign that cigar smokers are not constrained by conventional rules.

▪ PLANT

Tobacco (*Nicotiana tabacum*) plants are usually four to six feet tall. Native to South America, they have large arrowhead-shaped leaves and pink flowers. Plants are seeded in nurseries with differing degrees of protection depending upon weather and location. Seedlings are transplanted to open fields between October and the beginning of April. The leaves' aroma and taste increase as the plant grows. Cuban growers have given names to the leaves that are picked at various stages, usually week by week. *Libre de pied* are the first and least flavorful, followed by *uno y medio, centro ligero, centro fino, centro gordo,* and *corona*. The largest unblemished leaves with an oily and velvety texture are used to make quality cigars.

▪ Price

There's a price to pay for every passion, and the great cigars made from the limited supply of great tobacco reflect this. The simple law of supply and demand dictates that premium cigars must be expensive. From rolling* to sorting, cigar tobacco fabrication is executed by skillful hands, which also have their price in time and labor. But by the time a cigar reaches the consumer taxes on every level—from the international to the most local—account for a large share of the cost. This is why prices can very greatly from country to country or even in different states and cities of the United States.*

Havana cigar club, Paris.

■ Principles of Enjoyment

A cigar's taste depends upon the effect of smoke* upon the taste buds and receptors in the nose. Molecules must be soluble in order for perception to occur when they penetrate the liquid layer protecting olfactory sensors. The olfactory center of the brain contains twenty-five million neurons for interpreting data. Cigars only affect a fraction of these because tobacco is a relatively homogenous material. In a particular variety of tobacco, differences in flavor derive from the location of the leaf relative to the ground and the amount of exposure to sunlight. The first impression one has of a cigar is olfactory, a product of its aromatic molecules and the nicotine released upon lighting,* suspended or aerosolized within the smoke. The combination of these elements imparts a smoke with a distinctive taste, whether smooth, full-bodied, woody, etc. (See Vocabulary.)

Strong (or intense) smoke can still be rich or poor, and a rich smoke can be well or poorly balanced. While lasting power is an important and sought-after quality in perfumes and colognes, no matter how agreeable it may be at the outset, persistence is actually a defect for cigar smoke. Cigar smoke decomposes quickly, and generally without any improvement to the scent before dissipation.

Some sought after flavors include camphor, caramel, cocoa, cinnamon, earth, garlic, green pepper, honey, licorice, musk, pine, truffle, and vanilla—which can approach such undesirable odors as civet, burnt paper, or soap. Distinguishing between these and the many other possibilities takes much practice.

The following, based on Gilbert Belaubre's classification, may be considered a basic flavor guideline. Havana cigars are the most intense, and the most rich or luxuriant, whereas Dominican cigars are full-bodied and rich. Mexican cigars are light, and Honduran cigars are even lighter; Jamaican cigars are uncomplicated, but occasionally spicy or bitter; Nicaraguan cigars have fine body and aromas; Brazilian have less body but a variety of aromas; Philippine cigars are poor and sharp, and, finally, Java cigars are light, balanced, and slightly bitter.

■ PRODUCTION OVERVIEW
Plant to Puro

Havanas and all other great cigars are handmade. In Cuba, tobacco leaves are harvested between January and March, individually, in accordance with each leaf's maturity. After initial sorting, the leaves are placed in the *casa de tobaco* (tobacco hut) for drying and the first fermentation.* They are then sorted again, bundled in sheaves, and sent to facto ries to be selected by official State buyers. In the process, the leaves go through a second fermentation from re-humidification designed to show them to their best advantage. In the factories, they are aired out and then re-hydrated for their third fermentation within wooden casks. The third fermentation can last from a few months up to a decade, depending on specific conditions and circumstances. After being removed from the casks, leaves are blended. Blending* is one of the most crucial steps in production, a cigar's flavor depends on it. Next, tobacco leaves are stripped* to remove the middle vein from each leaf, and given to rollers* who craft the cigar by hand. Rollers are the elite in the cigar factory hierarchy. Armed with a handy *chaveta*, a steel tool* used to cut the wrapper and craft the head piece, they set about creating their masterpieces, each one unique.

Ernesto "Che" Guevara. Poster from a photograph by René Burri, Cuba, 1963.

■ Revolution and Production

The world of cigar smoking was radically altered when Fidel Castro took power in Cuba in 1959. A large percentage of the premium tobacco producers—many of whom were Americans with connections of various sorts to the overthrown dictatorship of Fulgencio Batista—fled, along with their know-how and large portions of their personnel. His communist beliefs (and some claim resentment as well) led Castro to immediately suppress all cigar brands.

Che Guevera, the Latin American strategist of guerilla warfare and one of the principal architects of the Cuban Revolution, was minister of industry in Cuba until he left office in 1965 to devote himself to international guerilla activities. As a staunch believer in Latin American cultural and economic integrity, he stressed that "sugarcane and coffee come from the exterior. They were imposed on us by the colonizers . . . But tobacco is ours and always has been." Nevertheless the names of all the traditional brands disappeared with their fabrication, and state-controlled Siboney cigars were invented, named after a hero of the Revolution. Unfortunately, interest outside Cuba in the four types of nationally sanctioned and mediocre Siboney Havana cigars was minimal indeed. With the massive decline in exports, Castro decided to change course completely. Small *fincas** were then given back to growers, and the state held on to only the giant plantations which had belonged to the "traitors of the Revolution." Castro then consulted

Zino Davidoff* on the problem. Davidoff advised a restoration of old brands and models.* It took Cubatabaco, the state managed tobacco concern, from 1960 to 1965 to produce cigars comparable to those made before the Revolution. Cohibas were also born at this time. Although this was about a year after Guevera left the government, his perspective was in a sense respected since the name Cohiba derives from the indigenous Taino word for tobacco or cigar. For about fifteen years, while a variety of cigars were available for export (notably by Davidoff and then Montecristo*) Cohibas were produced exclusively for Cuban government officials (see Cuban Brands).

Ring

According to legend, cigar rings, the bright paper bands on many cigars, were invented by eighteenth-century precursors of the dandies.* In his *History of the Havana,* Zino Davidoff* explains that they rolled a strip of paper around their cigars to protect their fingers and gloves from staining. But the official father of the cigar ring was Gustave Bock, a Dutch cigar merchant who in 1850 began affixing bands to the cigars he sold as a sort of publicity reminder to his customers. The idea caught on among manufacturers who sought to distinguish themselves from their competitors, and on 25 October 1884, the cigar ring was adopted officially by the tobacco factories of Havana. Ever since, cigar producers have tried to outdo one another's rings, with red and gold as consistently favored colors. The rings are placed on cigars before boxing and, like every

step in the making of Havanas, this is done by hand. The rings are affixed with plant-based adhesive and must be uniform in height to make for perfect alignment in the box.* Vitophiles (literally, cigar lovers; see Vitola) around the world collect cigar rings. Rings from nineteenth-century brands, no longer made today, are highly sought after.

Ring gauge, or RG, is the measure used in the United States, the United Kingdom, and Canada to specify a cigar's diameter. It is measured in sixty-fourths of an inch. For example a 48 RG is 48/64 of an inch, or three quarters of an inch (0.9 cm). A ring gauge is also the name of the metal or wood measuring device with holes of different sizes that is used to measure a cigar's diameter and to assure the diameter's consistency along its length (see Tools).

Rings being put on Havanas, in Cuba.

Rolling and Rollers

Cigar fabrication is, properly speaking, rolling, and rolling consists in nine extremely precise operations done by hand. The first stage concerns the filler (see Composition). The person who does the rolling, naturally enough known as a roller, or *torcedor,* works the three leaves (or several strips for lower quality cigars) that make up the filler together in his or her hand, and massages them into a cylindrical shape. The filler is then rolled into the one or two leaves that comprise the binder; together these are known as a "bunch." The bunch is then trimmed to the proper length. At this stage of development, they are known as *muñecas,* or dolls, by those in the trade. After having been stretched and trimmed, an operation that is essential in making a cigar look right, the wrapper is rolled around the doll, but turned in the opposite direction. The body of the cigar is now finished. The head is then cut and fashioned; left flat or made round or pointed, depending on what kind of cigar it is. Round and flat heads are made by attaching a small piece cut from the previous step of wrapper trimming. To give it the right texture, the surface of the cigar is then usually treated to finishing touches with the blunt sides of the *chaveta* (see Tools) and additional rolling over the wooden board which is another piece of the roller's equipment. The filler is also pulled and positioned from inside the wrapper, to assure cohesiveness and regularity of shape and smoke. The cigar is then cut to the right length at the foot (sometimes also called the tuck), and the diameter and shape is checked with a *vitola* (see Tools). These steps require the know-how and dexterity that can only be acquired after years of training, and which give *hecho a mano* (handmade) cigars the quality and appearance that machine-rolled cigars can only hope to emulate.

Romeo y Julieta

The Romeo y Julieta brand was founded in 1850 by Inocencio Alvarez and Manin Garcia. Its headquarters are still located in Old Havana's Calle O'Reilly, as is the equally renowned Partagas factory. Both headquarters are also great tourist attractions—something that makes them even more dear to the Cuban government, despite their

From top to bottom: rolling filler inside of binder; rolling binder inside of wrapper; the making of a cigar's head.

Following double page:
Inside a Cuban cigar factory.

Romeo y Julieta cigar boxes.

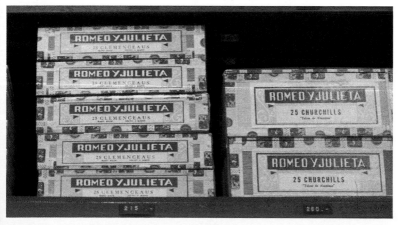

Claude Lorrain. *Seaport at Sunset,* 1639. Musée du Louvre, Paris.

pre-revolutionary history and status. The millionaire Jose Fernandez Rodriguez, known as Pepin Fernandez, had a strong passion for Romeo y Julieta cigars. He bought the company in 1903, and it soon expanded tremendously due to his efforts. He even planned to purchase the home of the Capulet family (Juliet's family name in Shakespeare's play) in Verona! He almost managed to do so, but settled for putting a cigar stand in the shade of the famous balcony, where every visitor was offered a free cigar until 1939. Habanos S.A. now controls the production of the famous brand. Today's Romeo y Julieta cigars

still deserve their excellent reputation. There are about a dozen different models,* of which the Churchill* is probably the most famous, although Romeo y Julieta also invented the more or less standard Corona format, and were apparently the first to sell cigars under that name. Their Cazadores are an inexpensive and especially smooth smoking handmade cigar.

Sailors

Sailors played an essential part in the spread of tobacco smoking throughout the world. As the first to arrive on the original sites of production and consumption (see Discovery), they were also

tobacco became popular were in Spain and Portugal. Cadiz, Seville,* and Lisbon were ports that connected Europe with the rest of the world. The French took up tobacco sooner than the English, who did not arrive in Central America until the middle of the sixteenth century. However, English merchant sailors introduced tobacco to the Russians at the beginning of the eighteenth century.

■ Seal

Before being put on the market, what is known as the guarantee seal, or the seal of authenticity, is placed on each cigar box. Following a law enacted to impede counterfeiting in 1912, Cuban cigar boxes are sealed with a Havanas strip. The seal is green, with an insignia of the Republic of Cuba to the left and the image of a plantation with three palm trees and five (older boxes have nine) plantation workers to the right.

Despite these measures, counterfeiting continues. Clandestine factories produce tasteless imitations of the greatest brands in Cuba.* The lion's share of these operations take place in the Dominican Republic.* In an effort to protect their citizens, some European countries have added cigar sections to their customs and anti-counterfeiting brigades.

the first members of the Old World to take up smoking, enlightening landlubbers as they smoked their way through the ports of Europe. They usually smoked pipes, chewed tobacco, or used snuff—the latter two often being their only choice, since ship captains were sometimes prone to prohibit smoking as a fire hazard. The main reason cigars were not smoked beyond their place of origin was the poor quality of contemporary "tobacco sticks." They were made to be consumed upon rolling, were usually smoked by the roller,* and couldn't last long even if someone wanted to save one for later. The first cities where

El Laguito,
Pinar del Rio
Palace, Cuba.

Secret

For the cigar aficionado* who is lucky enough to visit Cuba,* a trip to El Laguito—formerly the marquis of Pinar del Rio's Palace where Davidoff* manufactured Habanos and where Cohibas are manufactured* today—is highly recommended. The problem is that the moment you arrive obstacles proliferate to keep you out. You may be told that visits only take place during other seasons, repairs are being made, and so on. Yet if you insist, you might succeed in entering, and it is definitely worth the effort.

But this is merely symptomatic. Cuban cigar history is rife with secrets. Well before the Revolution,* manufacturers kept their cigar formulas and contents secret, including where the tobacco came from and which tobaccos were used. It is as if the pure simplicity of a product comprised of tobacco within tobacco necessitated added levels of complication. Methods and information are more closely guarded now than ever. Cultivators do not know which factories will be working with their leaves, and precise blend* composition is not revealed. Rollers* are even sometimes kept in the dark about which brand of cigars they are actually making. The reasons behind such secretiveness most often remain concealed.

Seville

For nearly three centuries Andalucia's capital was also the tobacco capital of the world. All the European colonial powers maintained monopolistic policies which consisted basically in the colonies sending everything they produced to the "mother country," which in turn provided them with whatever it deemed necessary. Because of its protected position on the

Guadalquivir River and its proximity to the Atlantic, Seville became the royal depot for all goods arriving in Spain from the colonies in the New World. The famous Casa de Contratacion was the headquarters, where all the "Archives of the Indies" can still be consulted.

Tobacco from Cuba* and elsewhere arrived in Seville in the form of leaves. These were then made into consumer goods in the city, providing it with one of many sources of wealth. Snuff was the product of choice until 1676 when cigar manufacture* began. It was not until 1731 that the impressive royal manufactory was established, leading to the elaboration of the *puro*. The international popularity of the cigar began during the Spanish War of Independence (1808–14, which the English call the Peninsular War, and Napoleon considered the "Spanish ulcer"). Both the French who occupied Seville and the English who were primarily responsible for liberating it, took to cigars with gusto. At this point Havana had been manufacturing cigars that were not particularly impressive, purely for local consumption, and shipping tobacco leaves to Seville, for three centuries (see Havana History). But now they took over the lead in cigar commerce from Seville, and began exporting superior quality cigars.

François-Antoine Bossuet (1880–1889). *Seville*. Private Collection.

Cohiba and Pleiades cigars in all available sizes.

Size

Before the Revolution* nearly a thousand types of cigars were made in Cuba.* This number went down to four soon after Castro took charge, but it is currently up to half the original amount, and growing. Cigar models* are defined by their size in terms of length, diameter (also known as ring gauge or RG), and shape. From *microscopicos* to *immensas* and *gigantes*, the variations are endless. The *demi-tasse,* also known as the lady finger, is among the smallest. The most creative is probably the *culebra,* which is made of three cigars braided together.

A cigar's strength is not related to its size, but is a function of the ratio of size to diameter, as well as a direct result of the particular tobacco leaves used to make it.

Some of the great classics in various formats are as follows: Cigars with straight, parallel sides and closed rounded heads include the demi-corona, panetela (which is long and narrow), corona, Lonsdale, and double (or *gran*) corona. These cigars range from four and a half to nine and a forth inches in length (11.5 to 23.5 cm) with ring gauges of twenty-six to forty-nine (10 to 20 mm). Another size category is comprised of models with cylindrical bodies and pointed heads. These cigars include perfectos and piramides, sometimes referred to as cannon shells. They range from four to seven inches in length (10 to 11 cm) and have a ring gauge of thirty-two to over fifty (13 to 20 mm). Torpedo or magnum formats are cigars with rounded bodies that are pointed and closed on both ends. These were formerly a big-shot status symbol. They measure from five and a half to ten inches (14 to 25 cm) in length, and have ring gauges of forty-five to sixty-one (18 to 25 cm).

Smoke

Referring to the curious qualities of smoke, Samuel Johnson once wrote: "Smoking is a shocking thing—blowing smoke out of our mouths into other people's mouths, eyes and noses, and having the same thing done to us." Smoke is made up of thousands of constituent parts, nicotine and odors among them. The combination of these elements is what sets off the pleasure involved in smoking. The original inhabitants of Cuba, whose custom of smoking greatly surprised the first European explorers to reach the New World, considered smoke as something that joined the earth and the sky. According to them, smokers could fly with their smoke into the clouds.

Smoke delivers a cigar's flavor and aroma. As it moves through the bloodstream into the brain, nicotine produces the passing, ephemeral sense of stimulation, paradoxically mixed with relaxation, so cherished by devoted smokers of all kinds. Intense smoke can create an impression of satiety well before a cigar is finished.

A cigar's smell is comprised of a complex mix of odors. Some of them are fleeting; others are heavy and linger on. The smoke's scent develops and alters considerably over its brief existence, and ends in a sort of state of cold decay that is never pleasing to the human olfactory system. As a Zen warrior put it: "The end of a good smoke is a little saddening. In some regards, it's a bit like losing a best friend who had time to sit and listen."

Smoking Room

Some people dislike the imposing smell of cigars and pipes. In the nineteenth century, partly in response to this, the smoking room became popular in polite society. The smoking room is a separate den where smokers, generally men to the exclusion of women,* adjourned after meals to smoke in peace and enjoy manly conversation. Non-smokers, (in other words women) were left to sip herbal tea in another room. Smoking rooms were off limits for family use. Naturally, the smoke they retained was not considered beneficial to children.

Men's clubs in Britain and on the Continent were equipped with smoking rooms. Today, smoking rooms are rarely part of even the most luxurious homes. But it is more than ever necessary to separate smokers and non-smokers in public places, officially for health reasons. Particularly stringent regulations on the topic were adopted in the early 1990s in the United States and throughout European countries. The laws in New York currently forbid smoking in nearly all restaurants, except those that can pass for bars, or in bar areas. Smoking is also off-limits in the workplace, where there are no longer smoker's lounges, and in all manner of public places in general. At least New Yorkers can still smoke on the street, which is now illegal in some parts of California. With so many restrictions, smoking sometimes takes on the tenor of a revolutionary act; an affront to the current social order. Unfortunately, lighting up a cigar on the street corner is far less practical than smoking a cigarette or even a pipe outdoors. Also, it would look ridiculous. Cigar smoking demands quiet time and a calm spot. This problem is partly redressed by the presence of bars that cater to cigar-smoking customers.

■ SOUTHEAST ASIA

Burma, Indonesia, and the Philippines are the three main cigar-producing areas in Southeast Asia. Burma sets itself apart from the others by the fact that ever since tobacco was first grown there in the seventeenth century, Burmese men, women, and children have been staunch cigar smokers. This is in contrast to all other Asians, above all the Japanese, who traditionally smoked only pipes. The custom is still going strong. The Burmese smoke small, locally made cigars which are white or green in color because their wrappers are made of Assyrian plum tree leaves *(Cordia myxa)* instead of tobacco leaves. There are countless manufacturers of these handmade cigars. As is the case in some Formosan tribes (in Taiwan), women smoke the biggest cigars, of a size that the men consider unmanly.

Cigars from Manila,* in the Philippines, have been rivaling Havana cigars among Western aficionados* since

Tobacco plantation on the island of Java, Indonesia.

the nineteenth century. Today's two top brands are Alhambra and Flor de la Isabella. Their pungent flavor resembles that of Burmese cigars. Only the Flor de la Isabella brand is exported. The cigars come in twelve different sizes, and are sold in airtight humidor boxes of fifty. The most popular model* is the "elephant's foot." This unusually shaped cigar is large and rectangular at the foot, with a small, rounded cut head. It has a rough flavor and strong, lasting aroma.

Tobacco has been grown since the seventeenth century in Indonesia, formerly under Dutch rule. Java, Borneo, and Sumatra produce what is known as "Dutch cigars."* They are dry and pungent, either without any pronounced aroma, or scented by added Asian spices.

Three centuries of Dutch importing have made these cigars popular in northern Europe and elsewhere. Among the best of them are Zino Drie and Zino Jong.

A tobacco leaf being stripped.

Stripping and Strippers

Stripping consists in removing the tough central vein from tobacco leaves. The vein is too bulky to be used in cigars. Stripping is done by highly skilled women workers. These specialists spread the flattened leaf on a curved board held in place between their thighs, grasp the leaf stem between thumb and index finger, and rip it out with a deft movement so swift that it is barely visible to the naked eye. The removed stems are used as fertilizer on plantations. The image of the board curving between the thighs, which has been an object of fantasy and fetish in some minds, is apparently what gave rise to the idea that *puros* are rolled between maidens' thighs, and other flights of fancy related to the profession. True to romantic descriptions found in *Carmen* and elsewhere, the strippers seem to be a lively, quick-witted, musical, fun-loving, heavy-smoking bunch.

Tabaquero or Tabaquera

Tabaquero or, for women, *tabaquera,* is a Spanish word which refers to workers involved in making cigars in cigar factories with leaf blends shipped in from tobacco production centers. The leaves generally come in *tercios,* sheaves wrapped in palm leaves, or in barrels, after they have been treated. The leaves are then humidified and fermented.* Once this process is completed, the primary task of tobacco blending* begins. Blending is what makes for consistent quality and flavor in cigars. Blended leaves are placed in wooden casks and re-humidified.

After a waiting period of between a few weeks and several months, cigar workers who specialize in the steps of de-veining and rolling the leaves begin their part of the work. The leaves are removed from the wooden containers, and divided in two by the removal of their main, central vein, which is too rigid and thick to be used in cigar making. The task of de-veining is reserved for "strippers,"* always women. The profession is romanticized in songs and stories, the most famous of which is *Carmen,* based on the novel *Colomba* by Prosper Mérimée, and set to music by Georges Bizet in 1845.

Rolling* is traditionally men's work, though today women rollers outnumber men. *Torcedores,* literally "twisters," still retain their status as the elite in cigar factory operations. They perform the single most important task in handmade cigar manufacturing: rolling the cigar. The work requires years of training and skill, plus natural aptitude or talent. In Havana cigar factories, the room where cigars are rolled is often called the *galera,* as in the "galleys" where naval prisoners were sometimes made to row, from ancient times through the nineteenth century. This refers to the fact that in former times military prisoners in Havana were often put to work in cigar production. Today, a man is often paid to read aloud to the workers. Some say this is how the *Montecristo** got its name, as Dumas's novel *The Count of Monte Cristo* had proved very popular in the factories.

Tabaquero rolling a Havana, Cuba.

Using a *chaveta* to cut a wrapper leaf scrap for a mouth piece.

■ Tools

A key member of the cigar fabrication team (*tabaqueros* in Spanish) is the *torcedor* (cigar roller).* Besides possessing excellent manual skills, a *torcedor* employs two tools, a *vitola* and a *cheveta*. A *vitola* can be either a sort of wooden tray with hollowed sections corresponding to the shape and size of different cigars, or a ring* gauge with holes for checking and measuring cigars' diameters. A *chaveta* is an extremely sharp, curved knife with a short handle used by rollers to cut a cigar's *capa* (or wrapper, see Composition), to cut the head of the cigar, and to cut out pieces from wrapper leaf scraps to make a cigar's head. *Chavetas* are also used to treat the surface of cigars in the final stages of rolling.

▮ Transplantation History

Indigenous to the American tropics, and discovered by Europeans as soon as they set foot in the New World, tobacco was immediately transplanted throughout the world, to flourish under the proper climate and soil conditions.

According to some historians, in 1518 Herman Cortez, the Spanish conquistador of Mexico, presented tobacco seeds to Kind Charles V of Spain, who had them planted that same year. Others hold that it was Francisco Hernandez Gonçalo who brought the first seeds to Spain in 1570.

There is also uncertainty about the date of tobacco's first planting in Portugal. Many believe that it was introduced there by the Spaniard Hernandez de Toledo, who brought it back from his expedition to the Yucatan in 1520. Others maintain that tobacco made its debut in Portugal as a present to King Sebastian from the Dutch merchant Damien de Goes, who acquired tobacco seeds in Florida.

Tobacco's first appearance in France is equally controversial. Jean Nicot, after whom nicotine was named, was once

thought to have brought tobacco to France, but it is now widely agreed that it was actually the monk André Thevet, when he returned with tobacco seeds from a voyage to Brazil in 1556.

English, Spanish, French, Dutch, Italian, and Portuguese explorers and merchants soon had tobacco growing throughout their respective colonial spheres: the Americas, Indonesia, Turkey, the Near East, China, Japan, Angola, and Mozambique. Because tobacco growth requires optimally suited conditions, many of the attempts to cultivate tobacco in new climes naturally failed. It did take successfully in some areas, though, including Cameroon, which still exports tobacco today.

■ UNITED STATES

The United States of America has been producing some of the world's finest tobacco ever since the first plantations were started during the seventeenth century. Important tobacco-growing states include Connecticut, Florida, Virginia, and most of the states between them, as well as a few northern states, such as Pennsylvania, Minnesota, and Wisconsin. As far as cigar taste goes, America has traditionally been diametrically opposed to Cuba,* preferring green, sweet cigar flavors, often enhanced with added spices and aromas, which alter and sometimes entirely mask the tobacco's original flavor. Traditionally wrapper leaves are also highly treated and matted. Matting is a process that coats the leaves with tobacco powder, giving them a dull finish.

Connecticut has been an important cigar tobacco location from very early on. A decade before the Revolutionary War, General Israel Putnam, who had served in the British army in Cuba, brought a load of ready to smoke rolled "tobacco sticks" to Connecticut, whetting New England appetites. The first cigars *per se* made in the United States were produced in and around Hartford and Suffield in the beginning of the nineteenth century.

After the American Civil War (1861–65) cigar smoking gradually became more and more popular. One of the major American cigar plants was located in Conestoga, Pennsylvania. Conestoga cigars were accordingly nicknamed "stogies," a term which came to designate cigars in general. These cigars were also referred to as "shoe lace" cigars because of their length and unusual thinness.

The United States is the world's foremost cigar producer in terms of output. With the high cost of labor, American cigars are exclusively machine-made. The major production and plantation area is centered in Tampa, Florida, where Cuban immigrant *tabaqueros* first settled in the eighteenth century. The most popular cigars in America today are cigarillos,* which are mass-produced. Hav-a-Tampa is a best-selling brand of cigarillos. King Edward cigars are made in Jacksonville Florida. The American brand best loved internationally is Robert Burns.

Connecticut wrapper leaf production is the exception to the high-volume mode of the American cigar industry. Over a few thousand acres near Hartford, a handful of planters cultivate their tobacco with the utmost care and craftsmanship. For the past hundred years, these plants from Cuban seed, have been grown under protective tarps to produce the exceptionally smooth, light-colored wrappers that form the outer layer of some of the best cigars made in the Dominican Republic.* Outstanding Dominican brands with Connecticut wrappers include Macanudos of General Cigar and Altadis* models.

Tobacco field
in Statesville,
North Carolina.

■ Vintage

Just as with wine, vintages exist in the world of cigars. In Cuba,* tobacco production is divided over several regions whose leaves vary in accordance with the geography. From east to west, the tobacco-growing areas of Cuba are: Oriente, Remedios, Partido, Semi-Vuelta, and Vuelta Abajo.* Although the very finest among these regions, Vuelta Abajo was the last to be planted for tobacco cultivation, in the 1770s. Over the years, many experts have tried to recreate the conditions found in Vuelta Abajo, but no tobacco has succeeded in rivaling it yet. The very same seeds and soil, relocated in an identical climate, cannot produce the same leaves. The top vintages or *vegas* of Vuelta Abajo are San Luis and San Juan y Martinez.

Some major vintages outside of Cuba come from the Bahia region of Brazil,* famous for its black tobacco, and the United States,* especially Connecticut (see United States) which is highly reputed for its top-quality light tobacco.

■ Vitola

The term *vitola* (or sometimes, vitole) is almost synonymous with the word cigar. At first it designated the wooden gauge (see Tools) used to calibrate cigar size. Now it refers to the entire cigar itself, including the inside, the outside, and the cigar's qualities and defects, as opposed to format, which is a matter of dimension, length and diameter. But the word *vitola* is more precise than the word cigar, since in addition to formal characteristics it also includes the notion of brand. Thus it is the opposite of a generic term, to be used regarding the brand and the format of a particular cigar. So, indicating a particular cigar you might ask, "What is this *vitola*?" And you will get an answer like, "A Partagas Lusitania." *Vitola* can also refer to a particular producer's model* with a specific format, and commercial name. In any event, the relationship between *vitola* and brand is so strong that collectors of cigar bands and vistas (the inside decoration of cigar boxes) are called vitophiles, and such collecting is called vitophilia.

Cigar calibration, Vuelta Abajo, Cuba, 1990.

Vocabulary

A very large lexicon comes into play when describing the quality of cigars and the pleasures of smoking. Only wine tasters employ a comparably extensive lexicon. Strength, richness, balance, and staying power are the four elements by which a cigar is judged. A cigar's "body," that is its strength or intensity, depends on the combination of nicotine and olfactory detectable molecules within the smoke.* What is usually called a cigar's "richness" is a factor of the aromas within the smoke. "Balance" relates to the harmony of these possibly competing aromas. And staying power concerns the amount of time the cigar's aroma remains consistent and delectable before diffusing, becoming dank, or turning musty. Within these categories any term relating to flavor is possible, once again in relation to four primary kinds of taste: sweet, salty, sour, and bitter. These can combine with descriptors such as earthy, flinty, grassy, antiseptic, burnt, or specific tastes such as cinnamon, opium, vanilla, or butterscotch.

■ VUELTA ABAJO

Vuelta Abajo is to tobacco what Domaine de la Romanée-Conti is to Burgundy wine or what Château Petrus is to Bordeaux, a peerless champion. Most experts agree that this region produces the best tobacco in the world. Its forty thousand hectares (154 square miles, less than two percent of the surface of the island) in western Cuba near the town of Pinar del Rio, was founded by the Spaniards in 1774. Strangely enough it wasn't until that time that the Spanish, who had occupied the region since the beginning of the sixteenth century, and who enjoyed both smoking and turning a good profit on tobacco, discovered how great Vuelta Abajo was for cultivation.

Stranger still is the fact that others were well aware of this quality. French smugglers and pirates prowled the waters around these parts since the beginning of Spanish colonization, and apparently were profiting from the yield behind the Spaniards' backs. It was not until the international recognition of Havana tobacco* near the turn of the nineteenth century that the new generation of Vuelta Abajo tobacco stock came to be known and appreciated by all.

The soil is reddish, sandy, and extremely fine-grained, and the region's *vegas* (tobacco plantations or more usually the fields comprising a plantation) grow some forty percent of Cuban tobacco. The *vegas* that produce the best tobacco are San Juan y Martinez (Vega 12) and San Luis, (Vega 13).

Plantations that raise *capa* (see Composition) leaves are usually covered with immense stretches of white cotton fabric, called *tapados*. These are suspended at least 6.5 feet (two meters) off the ground by wooden poles, forming an interesting contrast with the lush browns, greens, and reds of the region. The *tapados* screen the tobacco plants* from the wind and the sun. Each plant is tied to the netting, keeping it straight while enabling the development of uniform color and texture through an ideal exposure to light.

Boxing Havana
Cigars, Cuba.

■ Warehouse Storage

Completed cigars are stored in
boxes.* Havana cigar boxes are
made of Cuban cedar, a porous
and odorless wood that is perfect for the job. In order to pre-
serve its precious contents in an
uncontaminated atmosphere,
with the correct level of humidity, the underside of the box is
always unadorned, bearing no
labels or *vistas* (inside cover
decoration). Remember, like all
living things, a cigar will die
from lack of air. This is why
tube and cellophane packed
cigars should be smoked soon
after purchase, although cellophane can be quite useful protection against the extreme
humidity* of tropical climates.
After being boxed, cigars are

stocked in warehouses (such as
those in the Port of Havana) to
stabilize their humidity. A
fourth fermentation* is undergone the summer after final
fabrication. Superior quality
cigars that are well stored, shel-
tered from heat, light, and cold
can last a good ten years or
more. Villar y Villar's famous
cigars could last considerably
longer.

■ Women

It is true that while cigar smoking has been looked down
upon in general by some soci-
eties for varying lengths of
time and with different levels
of contempt, it has nearly
always been considered outra-
geous for women, especially in

nineteenth-century Europe. The Pre-Columbian civilizations where cigar smoking originates are the exception to this rule. Though perhaps fewer in number than men, women have been smoking cigars as long as men have. Catherine the Great (1729–1796) was an avid cigar smoker. Some authorities credit her with being the first to put a band around a cigar, presumably to keep her fingers clean of tobacco stains. The otherwise staid New England blue-blood biographer and poet Amy Lowell (1874–1925) shocked her neighbors by smoking cigars and cursing in public. Nellie Melba, an Australian coloratura soprano, attributed her impressive vocal strength to cigar smoking. La Africana, which in 1878 became the first Cuban cigar factory to employ a woman, shipped its choice cigars to her. French novelist Amandine Dupin (1804–1870), whose pen name was George Sand, notoriously smoked up to seven cigars a day. Her notoriety lives on in the world's largest women's smoking association, the George Sand Society of Santa Monica, California. Outlaw Bonnie Parker of Bonnie and Clyde fame smoked cigars, as did the expert markswoman Annie Oakley. The Hollywood actress Lillian Russell reportedly smoked 500 cigars a month. They were only three-inch long cigars, but her daily average rivaled Winston Churchill's.* Other female film celebrity smokers include Madonna, who shocked television audiences when she smoked a cigar on *Late Night with David Letterman* in 1994, and Whoopie Goldberg, who has a preference for Davidoff* cigars and says she has been smoking since she was a teenager.

Maurice Sand. *Franz Lizst and George Sand.* Chinese ink on paper. Musée George Sand, La Chatre, France.

NON-HAVANA CIGARS

Brand and Models	Country of origin	Format	Taste
ARTURO FUENTE	Dominican Republic	double corona	Light and easy to smoke, with
Canones		double corona	rich aroma. Light to medium-
Château Fuente		petit corona	bodied. Very well made.
Petit Corona		grand corona	The Especial is one of the best
Corona Grande		double corona	of the brand and one of the
Double Corona		grand corona	best Dominican cigars,
Especial		churchill	highly aromatic and satisfying.
8.5.8.		corona	
No. 4		robusto	
Epicure		corona	
Superior Reserve No. 3		corona	
DAVIDOFF	Dominican Republic	double corona	A high quality selection.
No. 1		corona	Good aroma, but light-
No. 2		panatella	bodied. Smooth.
1000		demi-tasse	The 4000 is a slightly spicy,
2000		demi-corona	enjoyable smoke.
3000		grand corona	
4000		churchill	
DON CARLOS	Dominican Republic	robusto	Smooth blend. Well balanced,
Superior Reserve			but slightly weak.
FLOR DEL CARIBE	Honduras	corona	A respectable cigar. Not very
Corona		double corona	strong. Best in larger sizes.
Double Corona		robusto	
JUAN CLEMENTE	Dominican Republic	double corona	Very well made cigars.
Gargantua		corona	Pleasant smokes, but low
Corona		corona	on personality. The Grand
Fagot		demi-corona	Corona is a fine cigar,
Demi-Corona		robusto	sprightly, verdant and earthy.
Gigante		grand corona	
Especiales No. 2		grand corona	
Grand Corona		churchill	
Churchill		robusto	
Rothschild		double corona	
Club Selection No. 1		petit churchill	
Club Selection No. 2		churchill	
Club Selection No. 3		corona	
Club Selection No. 4		double corona	
PLÉIADES	Dominican Republic	double corona	A fine selection, smooth and
Aldebaran		petit corona	rich in aroma.
Antares		corona	The Orion is well balanced,
Centaurus		corona	with a captivating grassy taste.
Orion		robusto	
Pluton		churchill	
VILLA GONZALES	Honduras	corona	Rough and tough cigars,
Corona		petit corona	tending to be acrid in flavor.

HAVANAS

Brand and Models	Length	Ring gauge diameter	Taste
BELINDA			Mid-range Havanas.
Panatela	4 ½″	34	Generally good, but with incon-
Princess	4 ¼″	34	sistent body and richness.
Petit Corona	5″	42	
Corona	5 ½″	40	
Petit	4¼″	30	
Preciosa	4″	32	
Superfino	5″	39	
BOLIVAR			The Corona Extra is the top of
Corona Extra	5 ⅝″	44	the line of this robust, straight-
Petit Corona	5″	42	forward, full-bodied brand.
Lonsdale	6 ½″	42	Spicy, earthy, and strong.
COHIBA			Cuban national brand elabora-
Corona Especiale	6″	38	ted with attention to detail.
Lancero	7 ½″	38	Light-bodied with full aroma.
Panatela	4 ½″	26	The Corona Especial is one of
Exquisito	5″	36	the best on the market. Fruity,
Robusto	4 ⅞″	50	woodsy flavor with a taste of
Esplendido	7″	47	honey.
Siglo I	4″	40	
Siglo II	5″	42	
Siglo III	6″	42	
Siglo IV	5 ⅝″	46	
Siglo V	6 ⅝″	43	
FLOR DE JUAN LOPEZ			Fine, well-balanced, traditional cigars. Full-bodied and rich.
Panatela Superba	5″	34	Sélection No. 2 is an excellent
Corona	5 ⅝″	42	robusto, aromatic and moist.
Petit Corona	5″	42	Highly enjoyable.
Sélection No. 1	5 ⅝″	44	
Sélection No. 2	4 ½″	50	
FLOR DE RAFAEL GONZALEZ			A venerable brand. The Lonsdales and the Petit
Lonsdale	6 ½″	42	Coronas are often very good
Panatela	4 ½″	34	cigars, well made and subtle,
Petit Corona	5″	42	with lots of taste.
Cigarrito	4 ½″	26	
FONSECA			A low-key brand. "Summer"
Fonseca No. 1	6 ½″	44	cigars, mild and light. Good for
Invicto	5 ⅜″	45	beginners, especially the Cosaco.
Cosaco	5 ⅜″	42	Smooth burning.
K.D.T. Cadetes	4 ½″	36	
Delicias	4 ⅞″	40	

HAVANAS

Brand and Models	Length	Ring gauge diameter	Taste
LA GLORIA CUBANA			Traditional Havana taste.
Médaille d'Or No. 1	7 ¼"	36	On the light side, but full
Médaille d'Or No. 2	6 ⅝"	43	of aroma. The Médaille
Médaille d'Or No. 4	6"	31	d'Oro No. 2 is a top-quality
Sabrosos	6"	42	Churchill, heady and fruity,
Tainos	7"	47	but never overbearing.
			Dominican (REM: blend).
HOYO DE			
MONTERREY			A top Havana, made with
Hoyo des Dieux	6"	42	attention to detail. Flavorful
Hoyo du Gourmet	6 ⅝"	36	and full-bodied. The Hoyo
Hoyo du Roi	5 ½"	42	des Dieux is a truly great,
Hoyo du Prince	5"	40	smooth-burning, well-
Hoyo du Dauphin	6"	38	balanced corona.
Palmas Extra	5 ½"	40	
Épicure No. 2	4 ⅞"	50	
MONTECRISTO			The world's best-selling
Joyitas	4 ½"	26	Havanas. Irregularities due
Montecristo No. 1	6 ½"	42	to the volume of production.
Montecristo No. 2	6 ⅛"	52	Great body and rich flavor.
Montecristo No. 3	5 ⅝"	42	No. 2 is packed and power-
Montecristo No. 4	5"	42	ful, for the real aficionado.
Montecristo No. 5	4"	40	
Montecristo Especial No. 2	6"	38	
Montecristo Especial	7 ½"	38	
PARTAGAS			Very old, respected brand,
Belvedere	5"	39	considered the standard of
Chico	4 ⅛"	28	fine cigars in Havana. The
Petit Bouquet	3 ⅞"	37	big models are well-built,
Corona Senior	5 ⅛"	44	tough, and subtle. The Series
Partagas de Partagas No. 1	6 ⅝"	43	D No. 4 is strong and spicy,
8/9/8	6 ⅝"	43	with outstanding aroma and
Lusitanias	7 ⅝"	49	body.
Series D No. 4	4 ⅞"	50	
POR LARRANAGA			Old brand, not very
Montecarlo	6 ⅛"	34	popular today.
PUNCH			A fine, well-balanced line.
Palmas Reales	5 ½"	40	Body and rich flavor.
Margaritas	4 ¾"	26	Punch Punch is an outstanding
Punch Punch	5 ⅝"	46	corona: spicy, strong, and
			balanced.
QUAI D'ORSAY			A handsome line, rich and
Corona Claro	5 ⅝"	42	aromatic. The Grand
Grand Corona	6"	42	Corona is straightforward
Imperiales	7"	47	and earthy.
Panatela	7"	36	
QUINTERO			Rough-crafted cigars.
Panatela	5"	36	
Purito	4 ⅛"	28	

H A V A N A S

Brand and Models	Length	Ring gauge diameter	Taste
EL REY DEL MUNDO			Old brand with a surprising
Corona de Luxe	5 ⅝"	42	range. Stronger on body
Choix Suprême	5"	48	than richness. The Choix
Demi Tasse	3 ⅞"	30	Suprême is a light, aromatic,
Grand Corona	5 ⅝"	46	enjoyable robusto.
Grandes de Espana	7 ½"	38	
Lonsdale	6 ½"	42	
Elegante	6 ⅞"	27	
Tainos	7"	47	
Petit Corona	5"	42	
ROMEO Y JULIETA			A top brand. Rich, strong,
Cedros de Luxe	5"	42	well-made cigars. One of
Churchill T/A	7"	47	Havana's finest. The Chur-
Petit Julieta	3 ⅞"	30	chill T/A is exceptionally rich
Regalias de Londres	4 ½"	40	and powerful. For seasoned
Sport Largos	4 ½"	34	aficionados.
Mille Fleurs	5"	42	
Petit Princess	4"	40	
Petit Corona	5"	42	
Corona	5 ⅝"	42	
Chico	4"	28	
Belvedere	5"	39	
Coronita	5"	40	
SANCHO PANZA			Excellent brand, not widely
Sancho	9 ¼"	47	available. Among the greatest
Molino	6 ½"	42	Havanas. The highly aroma-
Non Plus	5"	42	tic Molino is one of the best
Belicoso	5 ½"	52	coronas on the market.
STATOS DE LUXE			Rough, straightforward
Brevas 1 Mazo	5 ½"	40	cigars. Short on staying-
Selectos	5 ½"	40	power.
H. UPMANN			Old brand. Extensive range.
Aromaticos	5"	42	Less popular these days.
Corona major T/A	5 ⅛"	44	
Majestic	5 ½"	40	
Petit Upmann	4 ¼"	30	
Preciosa	4"	32	
Regalia	5"	42	
Épicure	4 ¼"	34	

T A B L E   O F   F O R M A T S

	Ring Gauge	Inches		Ring Gauge	Inches
Panatella	26	4 ½–4 ⅞	Grand corona	44–46	5 ⅝
Demi tasse	30–32	3 ⅞	Churchill	47	7
Petit corona	42	5	Robusto	48–50	4 ⅞
Corona	42	5 ½	Double corona	49	7 ⅝

I N D E X

SELECTED BIBLIOGRAPHY

Bati, Anwer. *Cigar Companion: a Connoisseur's Guide.* Philadelphia: Running Press, 1995.

Collins, Philip. *Cigar Bizarre: an Unusual History.* Los Angeles: General Publishing, 1997.

Hoff, Mark. *The Cigar Book: Up In Smoke!* Kansas City: Andrews and McMeel, 1997.

Hyman, Tony. *A Handbook of American Cigar Boxes.* Elmira, NY: Arnot Art Museum, 1979.

Lande, Nathaniel. *Cigar Connoisseur: an Illustrated History and Guide to the World's Finest Cigars.* New York: Clarkson Potter, 1997.

Le Roy, Bernard, and Maurice Szafran. *The Illustrated History of Cigars.* Paris: Flammarion, 1993.

Petrone, Gerard. *Cigar Box Labels: Portraits of Life, Mirrors of History.* Atglen, PA: Schiffer Publishing, 1998.

Shanken, Marvin. *The Cigar Aficionado's Art of Cigars.* Philadelphia: Courage Books, 1998.

Photographic credits: BARCELONA, Ymoda/Joseph Hunwick 10, LIÈGE, Museum of Wallon Art 80–81, LONDON, C. Beaton / Imapress / Camera Press Ltd 16–17, NEW YORK, Bettmann Archives 30, PARIS, Flammarion Archives 24, 25, 40, 60, 72 bottom, 75 top, 79 top, 85, 93, Bios/Henry Ausloos 105, Jean-Loup Charmet 110, Christophe L. 42, Coprova/B. Richebé 104–105, Dagli Orti 29–30, 32–33, 55, 56, 66, 72–73, 77, J.-P. Dieterlen cover, 31, 51, 74–75, 78, 92, Jacana/Jacques Brun 26–27, Magnum/Henri Cartier-Bresson 15/Fred Mayer 19 /Eliott Erwitt 20 /Dennis Stock 29 /Léonard Freed 34, 101 top /Ara Guler 45 /Philippe Halsman 47 /René Burri 53, 95, 98–99 /Sebastiao Salgado 63 bottom /Rio Branco 76 top /Harry Gruyaert 100 /Abbas 108–109, Musée de la Seita 35, 62 /Jack Burlot 6, 41, Réunion des Musées Nationaux 22–23, Harlingue-Viollet 43, Thomas Senett 76 bottom, Sygma/J.P. Laffont 12–13, 39, 52, 64–65, 90–91, 97 top, 97 middle, 97 bottom, 102 bottom, 106 top /P. Robert 67, 86–87, 111, 112–113, Marc Walter 28, 89 bottom, VANVES, Explorer/Jacques Brun 36–37, 69 /FPG International 46/P. Delance 63 top /P. Le Floch 68 top /J.M. Loubat 88 /J.L. Charmet 89 top, 101 bottom /E. Brenckle 94, Gamma 38, 45 /G. Noël 4–5 /Jack Burlot 48–49, 58–59 /Tounig Spooner 48 /Magnani Liaison 50 / François Darmigny 54 /Alistair Spoon 57 /Pete Souza 60–61 /Christian Vioujard 68 bottom, 102–103 / Rafaël Woolmann 84 /A. Mingam 96, Giraudon 79 bottom /Lauros 70–71, 82, 109 bottom /Bridgeman 106–107.

Translated and adapted from the French by Chet Wiener and Stacy Doris
Adaptation and additional research by Kathryn Lancaster
Copy-editing: Christine Schultz-Touge
Typesetting: Claude-Olivier Four
Color separation: Pollina S.A., France

Originally published as *L'ABCdaire du Cigare* © 1996 Flammarion
English-language edition © 2001 Flammarion

07 08 09 10 5 4 3 2

ISBN: 978-2-0801-0643-8
Dépôt légal: 10/2001
Printed and bound by Pollina S.A., France - N° L43868